SACRED CODES

CODES

IN TIMES OF

CRISIS

SACRED CODES IN TIMES OF CRISIS

A Channeled Text for Living the Gift of Conscious Co-Creation

NAOMI FAY AND NATHALIE MOUTIA

CORAL GABLES

Cover Design: Elina Diaz
Cover Photo/illustration: stock.adobe.com/Abbies Art Shop
Layout & Design: Elina Diaz

For permission requests, please contact the publisher at:
Mango Publishing Group
2850 S Douglas Road, 2nd Floor
Coral Gables, FL 33134 USA
info@mango.bz

For special orders, quantity sales, course adoptions and corporate sales, please email the publisher at sales@mango.bz. For trade and wholesale sales, please contact Ingram Publisher Services at customer.service@ingramcontent.com or +1.800.509.4887.

Sacred Codes in Times of Crisis: A Channeled Text for Living the Gift of Conscious Co-Creation

Library of Congress Cataloging-in-Publication number:
ISBN: (print) 978-1-64250-449-1 , (ebook) 978-1-64250-450-7
BISAC category code OCC019000, BODY, MIND & SPIRIT / Inspiration & Personal Growth

This book is dedicated to our children
Autum, Matteo, Holly, Micaela, Donovan, and Alya
and all the children in the world, big and small,
birthing more love for all those to come.

This book is encoded with the frequency and vibration of love and joy. It is a gift to humanity to understand and experience the mystery in its movement of creation energy. It helps transform over time all that holds you from knowing and experiencing your highest potentiality as a creator being. The high and pure vibrational frequencies held within this book help you to align to the truth of your divine nature. As you read and integrate the words coded in this book, spirals of rhythmic sounds and geometries are created to experience the mystery of creation.

Welcome to the journey as we travel this path together.

Buckle up and get ready for the ride!

TABLE OF CONTENTS

Foreword ... 15

Maneuvering Through Sacred Codes ... 19

Chapter 1 Sit into the Star Aligning with the Higher You ... 24

Power ... 26

Fully Receive the Light That You Are ... 26

The Beauty of Power ... 29

Discernment ... 30

Courage ... 33

Never Give Up ... 33

Transition from the Ego to Your True Nature ... 37

Some Mornings ... 38

Faith ... 41

Opening to the Profound Desire of Safety and Security ... 41

Prosperity ... 43

Your Choice ... 45

Determination ... 47

If You Strive, You Can Transcend All Limitations ... 47

Discipline ... 49

Meditate on Your Inner Gifts ... 51

How Can I Be of Service in Times of Crisis? ... 55

Chapter 2 Surrender Pray More, Plan Less ... 58

Innocence ... 61

Surrendering to Growth ... 61

Innocent Child Within ... 64

Emotional Traumatic Memories of Childhood ... 65

Living in Humility 67

    Fear 67

    What Is the Path of Humility? 71

    Forgiveness 73

Divine 74

    In Truth, You Receive All You Need 74

    You Are a Living Temple 76

    Asking Yourself Questions 77

Trust 79

    Trusting the Universe Comes to Ultimately
    Trusting Yourself 79

    Overcoming Doubt 82

    Surrender Is the Flow 84

Chapter 3 The Circle Starts with You Love 87

Love 89

    Opening to Loving Self 89

    Healing Process 92

    Caring for or Carrying Others 94

Security 97

    Through Adversity—Have Faith 98

    The Dance of Polarities 100

Harmony of the Heart 102

    Power Is Love 102

    Conscious Relationships 103

    Living More of Who You Are 108

Chapter 4 Transformation The River Flows 111

Wisdom...112

Profound Knowing...112

The Mirrors that Enlighten Your Consciousness.............115

Crisis, an Opportunity to Change.........................119

Flow of Creation...122

Finding the Balance by Managing Your Energy System.....122

Moving with the Flow.....................................125

Pressure of Time...128

Embrace Change...130

In a Time of Big Change..................................130

What to Do in Times of Great Challenges?................137

Can the Mind and the Feelings Be Controlled?...........140

Pure Light...142

Overcoming Fear...142

You Are Ready for These Times of Change................144

Fear of Fear or Negativity...............................145

Chapter 5 Expansion Wisdom of the Ancients...............148

Expansion..151

Leap into the Unknown....................................151

You Are Not Your Body, nor Are You the Mind............155

You Are Not Alone...157

Innovation..161

Embracing All—The Seed of Knowing.....................161

How You View the World Affects All Your Choices.........164

Moving into Your Channel.................................166

Reconnection...171

Aligning the Subconscious Mind to Your Consciousness 171

Saying "NO Thank You, This Is of My Past" 173

Interconnectedness 177

When All Seems Wrong 179

Chapter 6 Co-Creation The Song of the Stars 183

Success 188

Opening to Success 188

How to Avoid Creating Blocks 190

What Is the Purpose of Your Human Self? 193

Motivation 196

Living the Experience Fully—It Is Never Too Late 196

Choosing to Bring Joy into Your Existence 198

Focus on Being the Expression of Your Soul 199

Creativity 203

Open to Receive 203

Cycles of Creation 207

The More Programs Dissolved, the More You Manifest
All That You Are 209

Abundance 210

Opening to the Space Within 210

Co-creation with the Universal Laws 211

Abundance and Money 214

Chapter 7 Wholeness 217

Generosity 220

Giving Thanks for What You Receive 220

What is Being Generous? 223

The Gift of Being Human 224

Balance 226

Making Time in Your Day to Do What Your Soul
Asks You to Do 226

Balancing Body, Mind and Spirit 230

Living in Presence 233

Physical Strength 234

Letting More of Your Light Come Through 234

Connecting Your Heart to Your Head 239

Managing Your Energy Body—Yo\ur Precious Resource 241

Anchor Peace and Harmony 245

Changing Your Life by Loving Your Body 245

Belonging 247

Merging—The Three-Fold Flame 249

About the Authors **252**

FOREWORD

I have always wished that the Western world would teach its children at an early age the basic survival skills for our ever-changing and chaotic world. Skills that support our emotional, mental, and spiritual needs and connect us deeply with the natural world in which we live. Instead, as children we are taught how to be successful in a competitive and materialistic world that is fast becoming unsustainable. Yet we are never given the tools for when things are not going the way we think they should or when we cannot find the way to create a pathway to peace and compassion.

In times of inevitable change, we often experience fear and go into reaction because we do not know what to do. This is because we do not have the skills to navigate the changing world when things go "wrong" such as loss of job, loss of loved ones, ill health, relationship break-ups, and an ever-increasing stressful world filled with information overload that becomes more and more demanding every day.

I was thrilled to have been invited by Nathalie Moutia and Naomi Fay to write the forward for their wonderful book called *Sacred Codes in Times of Crisis*, which offers you, the reader, the tools you need for mind, body, and spirit balance and well-being.

I know from years of watching my students all over the world grow and enlighten that these beautiful words of wisdom will become a guide for you that, if practiced daily in your life, will sustain you and help you to navigate the difficult passages in life that may arise in the coming times.

For a teacher, there is nothing more rewarding than to see your beautiful students flex their wings and fly free to find their own way and share the beautiful gifts they have discovered in themselves during our time together. This is how I feel when I see the wonderful work that Nathalie and Naomi have created with this book.

This book is such a gift to humanity as these two beautiful souls share all their keys and wisdom with you. It is now up to you, dear reader, to open your heart to receive the wise and supportive gifts and keys they offer to you from their loving hearts.

I have watched Nathalie and Naomi grow and evolve over many years as they discovered and opened to the amazing souls that they are. It is not simply something they have created on their own. All that they share with you of their wisdom and heartfelt love are the keys and gifts their souls have carried for eternity. The gifts they are sharing with you, dear reader, also include the journey they themselves have walked to open to this amazing discovery that always sat deeply inside of them just waiting for them to arrive and open the gift box of their own being. And so too, dear reader, it will be the same for you if you allow it.

For this is always the gift for the teacher. It is such a gift to watch your students discover not what you have given to them but what they already hold inside of their hearts, even more so when you watch them open these gifts and share them with others.

This is the perfect co-creation between a teacher and their student. When this occurs, you know you have done what you have been guided to do and all is complete. For there is truly nothing you may teach a student but what they already know deep inside of their hearts.

I feel this is exactly what Nathalie and Naomi are now sharing with you, dear reader, and I know it will be a wonderful journey for you as you embark on a self-discovery tour of who you are—a beautiful soul filled to the brim with wisdom and love.

For how can you be anything else? You cannot. Anything else is simply a creation of your ego and mind in illusion. You can choose to live this illusion as your truth, because this is the choice you have, or you cannot. It is that simple.

The tricky part, of course, is making the right choice for you. Yes, you are opening Pandora's box when you take this mystery tour into yourself, but, oh, what wonderous gifts you will find. Yes, there will be a few challenges along the way, but Nathalie and Naomi have prepared your toolbox and given you all you need to find your way through the maze to the diamond at the center—you.

In this book, there are many keys and tools for you to use along the path you have chosen to walk. Be kind and gentle with yourself and others as you take this journey. Open your heart as wide as you can and receive as much as you can. Accept and know you are loved and supported and allow yourself to be nourished and guided by Nathalie and Naomi as they share their journey of growth with you. If you wish to grow and discover your divine truth, you could not have chosen two better guides.

I wish you well along the path. Blessings to you.

Ineasa mabu Ishtar

www.ishtarmasterchannel.com

MANEUVERING THROUGH SACRED CODES

Beloved Ones,

The Divine plan is unfolding even when you do not realize. Trust that when you listen to your heart's desires, your soul will lead the way. To maneuver through the chaotic nodes of creation, one must slow down and allow the divine plan to unfold.

The divine plan does not need to be rushed. Let go and allow the flow of the universe to support you by bringing in awareness and intention to your choices and actions. In turn, you allow time to ponder without the toughness of the mind or the tendency to control because you fear the unknown. Instead, allow the mind to relax as the body feels into the vibration of what truly matters to the heart.

For, in essence, this gateway is the tunnel of light that travels into the stellar light of your Sun. Within your core essence lives the brightest light, for creation energy is fueled by this light. Trust that your soul knows the way even when your mind does not and allow the timelessness of the moment to be the great epitaph. For each and every moment is a stepping-stone to the grandest plan needing to be discovered and played with your hands. Brilliance is in each step that you take with the willingness to know that you can play this tune over and over again until you are in the flow. In the flow, the mystery will be known within your heart of hearts, the gateway to your soul.

You are called to share the wisdom of your heart. You are called to share the gift of your light. What will you do now that all has slowed down and the excuses of the old do not pass muster in a time of deep change and crisis? For you are being called to gather up your resources and allow the new paradigm to be built upon what really matters to the soul instead of worrying about the ego's fearful ways of doubt. We are here to guide you through the troubled waters that you feel you cannot let go. The waters are here to nourish and replenish you instead of toppling you upon this great feat.

What really matters to you now when everything can be stripped away? Your core values and inner light is what will guide you upon these days. No longer can you look to another to do what you do not want to do, for it has never been the responsibility of another to find the joy within you. This is the only task of each individual heart to find and lead the way.

So, celebrate in this newfound place that all you really need is to know you. Come into this central place and bring forth the new. For everything can be created now without judgment and dismay. For everything has taken its toll of what we care others might say. You live for you and others live for them. Everyone has an experience to share upon this land. What is it that you are to really share to make your mark on this day? For everyone has their own gift to shower upon themselves and others in a new way.

Time to sing, dance, and create the grand festival of you. For you will now awaken all your gifts when you put down the efforts to withstand the judgments of yourself and the judgments of another, for the blame game is up and the new game is to commence. It is time to take a stand.

So, stand in the very essence of you. Be the giver and the receiver within the Divine plan. For everything requires balancing the energies of this land.

As you begin to harmonize with the sacred codes in this book, realize that you need not read it on a linear path. In this book, all sections are interwoven. It can be read in the proposed sequence, chapter after chapter, or it can be read otherwise.

And why is that? It is because life moves through the spiral; the experience of growth includes the repetition of what needs to be learned. You first need to see, accept, and release through the power of love and forgiveness.

Day after day, you learn from this living experience. This process may be sometimes painful, fearful, joyful, and blissful. It all has to do with the current of life that is vibrating in your cells. Having shut down your gifts, you live a life that is somehow duller than it should be, limiting the stream of creations in your body, and experiencing sometimes a very difficult life.

And how is that? That is because by refusing to be the co-creator self that you are, by closing your physical body to the sacredness of self, you are blocking the flow of creation. You are blocking the assistance from the Universe that is available all around you and waiting for you to call on for help.

This book invites you on an experiential journey to the self through the power of love, forgiveness, and grace.

Every section of the book is intended to expand your perspective and release the blocks in your life that keeps you from experiencing your highest potential.

So, we invite you to take this book in your hands, close your eyes, and breathe in the breath of life three times. Take this frequency and vibration into your physical body; as the experiencing of the words come, they will then be anchored in its most complete way through every particle of your body, touching your heart, body, mind, and spirit.

You may also place your attention on a part of your life that you feel you need assistance with the birthing of something new and allow your hands to open the book at the page that your spirit guides you to. This will be the message that your guides wish to share with you. Take time to read it once or more times. Read it slowly, feel it, sense it, reactivate the wisdom within and receive the gift of love as you move through this process.

Allow this message of love to nourish your entire body so that this truth of love may be yours. Gift yourself the assistance that is being offered to ease your day's experience. Allow spirit to enter your life and guide your way to serenity and wholeness.

Breathe in deeply in the present moment and allow all to be anchored in your physical body. Open to a new opportunity of change through grace and ease. As you close the book, give thanks for all you have received and go on with your day. Know that you are held and supported by the entire Universe and that you are not alone on this quest. Spirit is guiding you toward the fulfillment of living your dream. Welcome in passion and joy as it has the energy to push you forward to live your life as a powerful co-creator.

May this book accompany you on your journey of living your dream, so that pain and suffering may be lifted from this earth through the collective consciousness, enabling you to create a completely new world where love will be the experience for all.

SIT INTO THE STAR—Aligning with the Higher You

This code will help you repattern the limitations that disable the full opening of your heart and mind to who you really are. It allows the connection with the higher dimensions of you so that you may align with your soul and mission on the earth.

This sacred code activates your pillar of light within your energy field. This pillar of light runs vertically through your body which connects you to the heart of Source and all creation from above to the heart of source of all creation from below within Gaia, our Mother Earth. As your pillar of light is activated, you start to open to the energy centers within your body, enabling you to open through all the multi-layers of your energy bodies, entering the knowing and sensing of your multidimensional self. In this new awareness, you open to experiencing wholeness within the self as you connect with everything around you feeling one with all, bringing you on the path of love.

CHAPTER 1

SIT INTO THE STAR ALIGNING WITH THE HIGHER YOU

Beloved Ones,

As you sit within your heart, you start to listen to the desires of your soul, your wishes, your passions, your freedom, and your liberation. You start to wonder and then you sit, waiting for an answer. But we say that often the answer is not within the mind, but rather within your heart. Consider making choices throughout your moments with a new awareness where peace is at the heart, the axis point of all creation.

Come, now, and sit with us.

We are delighted to begin this journey with you, a path home. For today, we tell you of a story of what was once known long, long ago. For the time now is merging with the many planes of consciousness you hold as you walk along the rainbow bridge that leads you to the portal of one heart.

Many blessings are to be bestowed as grace does now come. Your willingness and strength have anchored as we braid the gifts of ever-present life and everlasting creation around you.

We ask you to come into the center of your heart as often as you can in the days to come. Building this knowing inside of you will align with your truth and allow you to trust as you walk along a path like no other.

You will break free from the shadows of doubt and arise into the sun, a symbol of the light within you. So, arise into your very light, Beloveds. But first, sit now with the knowing that all will emerge and soon you will be pulsed to share this with all.

For now, all the codes have woven within you and you now can connect the dots. The ancient One within you is ready to infuse all the gifts you once had to co-create something new. So, now a new cycle begins with the rising of the dawn. Let us now ignite with others and carry forth this light, for love's embrace is truly here. Love's embrace is here for you. Marry yourself and go deep within your very core by discovering more of the truth of you. So, what will you do to live this truth? What will you say? What will you sing? How will you live the gift? For all does converge into the one heart and now the song is to be sung with thy magic that comes from within.

POWER

FULLY RECEIVE THE LIGHT THAT YOU ARE

Have fun and create through form. Release that what you think must be or had planned it to be. If it does not happen, that does not mean that you do not deserve. It is simply because you are not in the flow; instead, you are manifesting through your limitations.

There is no lack from a soul perspective, it knows, it can dance; have fun with creation source energy. Remember that a part of you is always in this higher perspective. Your soul is creation. When you become this spiritual human that you are, when you live in the present moment consistently day-to-day, you create new levels of consciousness and higher frequencies. From this place, you can, in every moment, experience a new opportunity to explore and create. It is a constant flow. The future comes to you without asking or thinking about it. It can now manifest far beyond what you can imagine because it has accessed the unlimited potential of creation energy.

We ask you if you are ready to step out of the density that is created with the overuse of the mind, feelings of limitations and fear. As you allow yourself to be fully present, you experience the beauty and the harmony of the Universe, you satiate with the vibrational power of the present moment being fully alive in the now.

Release your need to figure out how to attract what you need, or to try to think how it will be in three months, or even how money will come. It cannot be figured out through the mind. All you need to focus on is opening your heart and lighten up. Do things that allow the body to open, soften, and feel good and get ready to receive the energy of creation that you are in truth.

Use your creative energy and imagine a golden field around you. Start to expand the energy and allow for any other colors of creation consciousness to merge through. Breathe and enlighten as you access the master within who enlivens into the present moment. More energy and light codes can pour through you, around you as you become One with all. Feel the flow of the mystery and experience your energetic code expanding all around you. You are a transmitter of creation energy. This energetic code is yours to learn and to relate to, for it reveals more of your gifts. Your task is to make manifest actively and consciously into your reality.

When you experience higher states of consciousness, you begin to live in the present moment. You are in bliss, for you expand your potential and feel the freedom and liberation knowing more of what is possible. Potentiality increases because you are open to more possibilities and you begin to experience your life as an adventure willing to explore and play with life itself. Your wonder and curiosity awaken as you are willing to live more spontaneously with vitality and excitement.

Let this be your prayer, to be One with your light. Pray more. Plan less. Let this be your devotion, to be One with your light. For it takes consciousness, Beloveds, to be an active co-creator of your experience. For truly this is what co-creation is, the embodiment of your light. Co-creation in consciousness allows your being to be filled with more light. Co-creation in consciousness allows your frequency and vibration to be the quotient of higher light.

For everything and nothing can be threaded upon streams of light that you may activate within your very life. Allow all your willingness to be in the presence of love. Allow and revel into your greatest gifts as you breathe into self. For as you bring awareness to your breath, you activate your soul's mission and purpose and are ready for your quest.

It is very simple, yet complex, when you are not present at first hand. So, we are here to remind you again and again to open, soften, and breathe as you take a stand. As you stop moving and doing unconsciously and rushing about waving your hands, you will then be able to focus your energies on conscious co-creation upon the land. In this newfound place of love, will you be able to renew what you do as others around you will wonder how you could do what you do.

For everything can move with flow when the mind and heart are aligned. Everything can be seen and experienced from the higher perspective of your soul. We are here to help you be the bridge of manifestations that are imbued in gold.

THE BEAUTY OF POWER

The beauty of power is what you are. It is not something that you need to strive for, nor does it have to do with physical rewards and material benefits that are provided in your world. This is the energy of the ego or the small self. The power we are talking about is the One that gives you a meaningful life, the One that gives strength and spiritual power.

When you dive deep within, choosing to discover self-empowerment through the power of love, you find infinite beauty. Breathe and feel this intimate place where you can reclaim your beauty, your innocence. This place is where you can birth your creations from a whole new realm of consciousness. When you find this in the core of your being, you will have the power to transform your life.

The more you exercise being in the now, the more you are willing to let go of your fears. You live life fully by embracing the moment instead of fearing the moment. Once you build up your awareness, you will discover that many of your choices were influenced by your ego and not your soul. The ego's job is to protect you because it fears the unknown, but once you tap into your soul's essence of love you begin to master the mystery of flow. No more will you fear the future or keep dwelling on the past. You will be instead be exhilarated to spontaneously live a life that makes you laugh. Your habits of old will dissolve away for it is something of your past. It no longer resonates with you for you are lighter and ready for the grand path.

The power of love that inhabits you will deepen the trust in yourself and with life. You will notice the beauty that is created around you and you will be willing to join in on the fun. You will be ecstatic and will want to share what you know. You will then be of service to others because that is the natural way the energy will flow.

Enter the powerful experience of love. Cherish who you really are and who you continue to become. Encourage yourself to trust the creator that you are. Transform the ego's power play into the power of play and love. Pure fulfillment will now be your experience because you unraveled the knots in our life and gained more ease and flow.

DISCERNMENT

You have held many beliefs and programs that humanity has experienced through much pain and suffering. You are part of the whole and the whole is part of you. The evolvement of the soul is also the evolvement of the collective and so to you light connects to all that is. On the micro level, you have held stories handed down from your parents as well as the community and environment in which you have lived. Story upon stories, the energy has compounded these beliefs for many years. You, in your unconscious awareness believed these thoughts, fears, and illusions as your own. During your young age, you stored all that your parents shared with you as if they were the words of God. Children are like sponges, as they take on all that is thought, said, and done. Sometimes even when you grow up, you pursue thinking that others know better than you, as you have not been taught to have faith in yourself.

The gift of discernment is something to exercise because only YOU can know what is best for you. All the others can think they know; however, it will always be from their point of view. Deep inside, you hold a higher wisdom that can guide you and show you the way. When you practice self-love and open your heart to yourself, you will profoundly reconnect to your intuitive gifts. Your truth will emerge and suddenly you will realize the ways in which you denied and sabotaged yourself.

As you initiate your intuitive abilities and open to your inner guidance, the messages you receive will not be doubted but rather acted upon. Despite whatever fear arises, deep down inside you know you must act. Your soul is pulsing you to move past complicacy and courageously live the life you dream. You will start the process of questioning all that you know, all that you feel and what beliefs systems are you attached to. You will then ask yourself, "Is this in alignment with my soul? Will this bring me peace and fulfillment?" Soon, you will gradually grow out of many limited beliefs and you will begin to free yourself from the confines that held you in stagnation, struggle, or burden. Along the journey, you might also notice that you will keep some beliefs thinking they are your truth, yet only to realize later that it was not fully your truth. You will begin to fine-tune your choices with discernment. You will refine your intuitive abilities and trust that no matter what comes before you, you will be able to confront and choose again to co-create the life you dream.

Practice discernment by noticing the difference between being and doing. Ask yourself what is required to bring more balance into your life. As you become aware of the patterns that you create, you begin to understand that you have the power to change them. Being and doing will become a dance that serves the soul and all of creation because it does not force or control. Instead, it moves along the cycles of creation in flow. Follow the mystery, follow the flow as you ease into the knowing that you are human soul.

All that you do, as the cycles of change move through you, you soon realize what is not for you and when it is time to bring forth anew. Start to imagine what your life can really be once you know what you have done and what can no longer be.

In the pause of being, you start to reflect. The messages of light bring peace to your intellect. Away you will go as you float on a stream, a stream of consciousness that brings forth your dream. The dream is made manifest for your actions are aligned with your heart. You build with your mind; you build with your heart. The synergy of one is harmonized with the two. The mind and heart are one with the passion of you.

The choice then comes down to choosing with love or choosing with fear. Which one will you choose, manifest and co-create or adhere to fear? As you come around the spiral of creation again, you will now have the wisdom to transform instead. Gratitude will take hold and you will know that you are blessed and that which you once took for granted will be a priority instead. For you know all your experiences have brought you to this point and you are empowered to create love in form and your reality is sought. What you bring forth is with consciousness, we say. Hey! Co-creators, are you ready to play?

You are life, Beloveds! You will always expand and grow. You are love, Beloveds! So, get ready for the show!

COURAGE

NEVER GIVE UP

Sometimes, things just do not happen as you wish they would. It is important to remember that when you have the impression that the world is against you and even though it does not happen as you wish, life is never against you! To master the flow of creation is to move with it, not against it.

Divine timing and purpose work with the flow of creation. So, take one day after the other and have faith that things will unfold. One thing is certain, things will happen as they must happen. You can do your best, act when needed, but to force is to create struggle and pain. When you realize that you are part of the whole, you can work with the universal energies of creation that flow with ease and grace.

In times of crisis, please remember that the entire universe is here to support you. Once you understand and integrate your newfound choices of love and higher light, you will manifest your dreams into your reality. Your very prayers and intentions are heard.

KEEP FAITH!

All will unfold; understand that conscious creation is a process for you to experiment with and refine. Your diligence will be needed if you are to understand the flow of creation, for you will need to practice this art as you integrate your choices with awareness and make it real for you in your everyday life.

Life has its flow, and you will learn to go with it like a river, sometimes there is more of a current, sometimes it is very still. The purpose is for you to let go, release your need to control, and accept what is to understand the universal flow of creation.

Listen to your inner guidance of when you need to act, reflect, and/or rest. You are the one to choose how you experience your creations. Are your co-creations going with the flow or against the flow of energy? The choice is always yours. The soul is pulsed to learn and grow no matter what circumstance. The difference here is whether you want to learn through pain and struggle or through ease and grace. There is no judgment. We are only here to remind you that you also have the power to choose because you are the master co-creator of your life. If you are unhappy with your choice, choose again. Your dedication and diligence to learning how you use your energy is required to co-create a life you intend.

Act when you are guided to do so. Pray, meditate, or ponder the inklings of your soul. If you intend to marry yourself and be in relationship with your higher self, you will be surprised by all that you already know. Relax your mind. Soften your heart. Stop all the chattering in your mind that you are no good. Clear, cancel, and delete all the negative self-talk. You are the master co-creator of your life. Believe it when we tell you, you have the power to light the spark. Ask for assistance if you need from your Angels and Guides and Councils of Light, but know that they are you and you are they in the collective conscious co-creation of life.

Ask for things to untangle in a blissful way for the good of all. Go out in nature and connect to Source. Remember the answers lie deep with your core and with the universal energies of life creation. Ground into Gaia, or Earth Mother, our home, feel her support and know you are not alone. Connect to the star's way above the sun. Expand out further into the great Central Sun. The light in creation is connected through all. Be willing to understand that you cannot possibly comprehend it all. It is only to be experienced and discovered through the unknown. Your faith and trust will throw you that bone.

Allow the unfolding of the divine plan and trust that your choice will be for the good of all. As you tap into the collective energies and understand the universal laws, conscious co-creation will be yours. As you become the master co-creator, you will entrain your energetic field to resonate with more and more higher wisdom of frequencies of sound and light. You will feel and know your connection to unlimited source creative potential. You are fueled by love and the power of your divine light.

So, breathe and have faith. Know that whatever comes your way you will be able to meet because you choose conscious co-creation, and you will continue to manifest your light. Stay focused. Do what you are guided to do. Accept what you cannot change. Be the life you dream. Dream your life into existence. All is well in conscious co-creation.

By opening your heart and having faith in life and others, you can receive and imagine new ideas and opportunities. Your commitment to yourself will expand. You will be focused and determined. And when you experience challenges, you will know that it is then that the greatest insights can be achieved. These will be the moments that you will remember that have fortified your trust in yourself and in the invisible forces that surround you. These will be the moments in your life when you have learned the most because you have consciously chosen to transform your old patterns of conditioning that kept you stuck and full of guilt.

Within the darkness, you are the light. So, take heed, the message is bright. Do not give up. For all that you thought you knew can now be surrendered and birthed into the new.

The mind softens after it is exhausted. When you finally let go of the need to control, the softening arises, and the heart feels and wants to be known. Allow the mystery of life to take hold. This is where the magic is born within the seeds of growth. The inklings of all creation start to stir, wiggle, and create a stream of conscious light. It is born in the darkest, darkest night and birthed into the light. A new code is born!

All is a game to be won in love. Stop all the chatter and be in love. The messages will come; just open and receive.

Receptivity is an art that one needs to believe. Allow the innocence of love to come. Forgive yourself all your worries and remember to have fun.

You all get caught up in the illusion that you are not enough. Beloveds, we are here to tell you, YOU ARE ENOUGH! YOU ARE ENOUGH! Sing it into your heart, and know it in your bones, "I AM ENOUGH."

TRANSITION FROM THE EGO TO YOUR TRUE NATURE

The transition is possible when you open yourself to the power that creates change. This can only be found when you live through your self-awareness and expand your consciousness. Your self-image is made up of all the moments you felt unworthy, not good enough, frustrated, and other times when you felt satisfied, loved, and worthy. The negative beliefs have the power to keep you in a never-ending cycle of repetitive pattering because of your fear of being hurt once again. Instead, you close your heart to yourself as well as to others.

Your habits, beliefs, and expectations are stored in your ego-self, as it always looks at life through the eyes of self, concentrated on satisfying its needs. The transformation through perspective of your self-image is pointless because it does not have the power to change; it can only reinforce its own self-image.

By realizing that your self-image is only a construct of the past and a projection in the future, you will see that the only way out is choosing to live in the present moment, as in this no-space there is no need of any self-image. You will then have no self-image to live up to.

Being present within the now is the place where the real power of transformation lies. It is not something that you will need to try to do, it is not through mental activity, is it through the vibration of the *beingness*, through the feeling of the feeling.

Sit and be knowingly in yourself, reconnect with your true inner nature where there is no fear nor doubt, as the past and future do not exist in the present moment. You will enter the timeless flow of the ever now, living through a creative field of awareness that will inspire you to change.

Do not judge the ego, rather observe and be aware of the ego and know and accept its purpose for you to grow. You have come to the earth to shine your light as you let go of density and lower vibrations of the old. You have come to remember and be empowered to transform the energies that no longer serve. Use the fuel of transformation and make room for a new story within your field of light, that will be unified instead of divided as you build a new way of life.

SOME MORNINGS

Some mornings, you get up and you just do not feel well. Why is that?

During the night, you travel through your unconscious, and, as you are always One with the consciousness of humanity, you sometimes wake up in lower vibrations and get the impression that it is yours. Should you start your day continuing to live in the unconsciousness and not fully aware, all will mirror back to you. Your day will be filled with old patterning that is waiting for you to remember that your true nature is One of light. You may feel powerless and wonder why you are having a bad day.

There are no bad or good days, they just are. As creator in your creation, you have decided, unconsciously maybe, that this day was going to reflect what you woke up with, which initially was not your conscious creation, but by not changing it, it became yours more and more throughout the day.

We wish you to understand that every morning the canvas of your day is white, cleared, and you enter your creation of the day. The flavor and colors with which you wish to create will be reflected without any judgment on your creation. This is for you to learn that what you hold as a multidimensional being creates the life in which you are.

So, we strongly suggest that you check if the frequency which you currently are holding is really what you want to create? Is this of service to you? What do you want?

When necessary, use any technique that is good for you to elevate your vibrations. You can meditate, you can dance, sing, anything that will elevate your frequency to the level from which you wish to create, gifting you new opportunities of more ease and grace in your day.

Be gentle with yourselves, Beloveds. In times of transition as well in your day to day, you will go through the waves of creation. Honor what has been created in the moment. Honor what you are feeling in that moment and bring awareness to it. What are you thinking? If your thoughts are tiring you, notice that! If you are getting tired of feeling the same old thing, notice that!

In the awareness lies the liberation to create something
new, yet we ask you to be gentle with yourself. At times,
seeing the blank canvas may need the facilitation of
inspiration. Inspiration will fuel the passion and express it
out in form. This is your creative expression waiting to form.
Honor it, do not judge it, and just allow the expression to
take form. Whether it is through a walk, a dance, an intimate
conversation with another or the divine, allow the creative
of expression of your soul to come into form.

Nature is the doorway to this inspiration. Take little steps
and allow the energies of love to support you even when
you wake. Some mornings, you may be mourning a loss and
feeling sad. Allow the repressed energies to arise for deep
transformation to take hold.

For all these emotions and thoughts do have a cycle too, to
transform back to the light and circle through you. Notice
what is your energy, what you have you created. Notice
what energy you adopted to not feel slated.

So, with this awareness, what will be the driving force for
your choices? Focus, focus on your awareness and see far
beyond the boundaries of the old and shatter them and
make you now whole. For all you really need to know, what
will you carry and what will you unload.

FAITH

OPENING TO THE PROFOUND DESIRE OF SAFETY AND SECURITY

The natural flow of desires is that they come in and out of your lives constantly, changing for no reason. However, some desires never change, like the desire of feeling safe and secure. There is a huge gap between the comfort of feeling fully secure and held by the benevolence of life and the doubt and anxiety of not feeling safe, even if you live in a secure environment. This gap can in no way be filled by external means, as this will only trigger even more for your ego which has the feeling of being less and doubts itself.

The deep inner security is something that can only be found through the connection with your higher self as you merge inside and discover the beauty of the magnificent powerful being that you truly are. By entering the inner peace that lives inside of you, you will discover this limitless power that provides you the strength and support to overcome any anxiety or doubt, activating deeply the sense of security and safety.

Activating consciously and grounding through your feet and body to the benevolent heart of the earth, opens you to the possibility of receiving what has always been waiting for you, but you thought impossible. Through the action of centering yourself, you can immediately release insecurity, doubt, anxiety, fear, or any feeling of disempowerment. You than allow the E-motion to move through you. You stop creating dramatic scenarios and you free yourself from the difficult experiences that bring a lot of imbalance and chaos in your life.

Remember to ask yourself if these fears are present in the now, or are they built from the past and projected to the future. In another words, pure illusion, creating a false chaotic sense of insecurity, pure fantasy. This powerlessness is not real, it only feels very real in the moment, so take a deep breath, center yourself, and tell these anxious thoughts that you no longer need them. By doing so, this imbalanced energy will dissipate on its own. Do not hang on what does not serve you.

Anchor an unshakable level of security and safety by centering yourself, connect with this immense power of creation within, and make sure you do not nourish undesirable and irrelevant thoughts and feelings that darken your experience with a shadowing effect that keeps you in the illusion of disempowerment.

Beloveds, we are here to provide you with the frequency and vibration of safety and love. In the energetic entrainment of these words, we weave the threads of light into your consciousness to illuminate your gifts and connect you to your higher light to remember your true divine nature. We are here to remind you that we are One in this light and we can together fulfill the dream of conscious co-creation on the earth.

PROSPERITY

You are the master of your life.

If you are not receiving all the prosperity you dream of, that only means that parts of you have shut down due to past experiences. As Mother Nature is abundant in all possible ways, you also are entitled to the same as you were birthed from the seeds within the womb of creation.

If you nourish the faith that the Universe is not against you, your false beliefs will start to undo themselves all on their own. It is not a process that happens through the mind; therefore, it cannot be controlled nor rushed. However, if you focus your thoughts and feelings on activating the faith and sense the energies of the invisible world around you, you start to open your beingness to receive the blessings that come your way.

It might not have the form you want; it might not come in the way you want, but it will enter your life as you have opened your heart and eyes in faith, allowing the unknown to be revealed. It is not that it was not there before, it is only because you could not perceive it that it did not manifest in your life. Prosperity is a given, it is all around us, it is simply because we do not attune to it, you do not believe in it, that you miss it.

So, allow yourself to have faith in yourself and in what life brings to you, as you are the vessel through which the magic of life can come. If you do not open to this possibility, you will not receive the prosperity that you dream of.

When you are called to sit, reflect, imagine, and connect with all that you are, you allow conscious receptivity to build and be attracted to you. Like a magnet, you will attract the vibration that you hold in your heart and by simply being you attract the very essence that you are. This is how you are to birth a Golden Age of unified light; for love's greatest gifts can be truly manifested into form.

When you sit, connected to this unlimited potential, it fuels the passion within you, pulses you to move, to choose, and to create into form. You start building from your root, the very center of your stability, as you know you are truly safe and secure because you have all that you need. You are unified and connected to the mystery of all that is.

To flow with the waves of prosperity, one needs to put hope in front of all things—on behalf of hope you will act and choose to create whatever will serve your highest good and the good for humanity. Do you see Beloveds? We are asking you all to manifest at a higher frequency of light by allowing and moving the cycles of creation. In the center point of these two cycles lies the heart of All That Is. In this center point, you may draw on the power of light and love to manifest your dreams. In the center point of light and love, you are at peace with the Beloved, the true home that you seek. In this place, the true north is revealed.

Many Star Elders travel into the center point of creation; for stars, planets, galaxies, and universes were birthed in the zero point of One. So, as you say, as above, so below, the prosperity of light is on the go. The prosperity of love fortifies the field to create a unity of light.

YOUR CHOICE

Spirit knows your name, knows your anxieties and feelings. Spirit is watching, waiting for you to take their hand. It is your spiritual choice. Through the journey of the soul in the experience on the earth, a wall has been created between you and spirit; however, we wish to remind you that you are never alone, your soul is filled with the love of source, the veil is inside you nowhere else.

You are currently opening to new states of consciousness, experiencing a quantum leap. You are seeding great hope, infinite love, clearing the old that no longer serves, rebooting. You are ready for this recalibration. Practice being what you choose to be, the more you become what you dream to be, the more you anchor your infinite self. Nurture yourself consciously on how you breathe, eat, and move.

Be willing to stand up and show yourself, to express the love that you are, inspiring all around you, enabling others to be more of who they are, whether they are conscious or not. Define what is important to you, and choose to feel it, making it your reality, choosing how you want to live and express your infinite love. Keep your center regardless to what is happening around you; choose to be an evolutionary influencer and way shower.

Continue to observe yourself as the multidimensional being that you are; your choice to incarnate love and abundance will have a ripple effect on your life and for those around you. Allow the chaos that is around you to bring up what you want to change, and see this as an opportunity to become stronger, ready to rise, more stabilized than before and focused on what you want to create.

And remember, you are not alone!

The belief that you do not have a choice is what needs to be transformed. All you need to do is to be willing to see a new perspective. You might have been fearful of making the wrong decision, you might have been fearful of the unknown and, therefore, instead of choosing, you have remained in the same pattern of what you have created.

Once you move through the fear of the choice, you are empowered to know that you can always choose again. When the choice does not give you a desired outcome, we say, choose again. This is how you learn to maneuver with the mystery. Do not stay in stagnation for fear of choosing wrong. Just choose again. Too many times you value the perfection of what your ego deems as appropriate. The soul knows that the perfection is within the movement of the energy and not the outcome. For life will continue to move and flow with the universal forces of love. Allow the energies of choice to be your teacher, dance, and find the balance within. The balance only happens in the dance. You cannot know what you do not experience.

You have been given the gift of free will to understand the process of creation. Allow your vision to move through your mind, your heart, and incorporate it in your thoughts. The mind needs the space to know that you may choose again, and the heart needs to feel safe in the unknown. Take time to tap gently on your heart center, bring your awareness back into your inner intelligence as your breath slows down the rhythm of your blood and choose from within.

Choose and choose again. Choose and choose again. Let this be your mantra as you learn to co-create the life of your heart's desire.

Here I sit
Here I ponder
And reflect what it is that I truly want.
Here I sit
Here I wonder
And ask
What have I created in conscious light?
Do I like what I see?
What choices did I make that took me to this place?
Here I sit
As wide asunder
In observation of my ego and higher self.
Who is this person that I have created?
What is the illusion that I believed?

DETERMINATION

IF YOU STRIVE, YOU CAN TRANSCEND ALL LIMITATIONS

So many of you, when talking about being human, refer to something limited. You say that nothing can be done, that nothing can be changed, that all is in God's will or a mistake from your ancestors. Living this way keeps you trapped and feeling powerless.

We wish to remind you that if you choose to open yourself to the possibility of what it really means to be human and become again the true powerful creator that you are, you will step out of all the limitations that have been set on you by your limited beliefs and conditioning. When you open yourself to your true nature, allowing yourself to be what human really means, the limitless possibilities that are offered can start to show up.

With the will to strive, you can transcend all the limitations, those placed on you through your ancestral lineage, your genetics, and ultimately your given nature. You have the possibility to go beyond your current state of awareness if you are willing to sail within into new places of your beingness. So, we encourage you to stay focused on your true nature, even if you cannot really know who you really are within, allowing yourself to go on a journey within to discover the eternal light that shines within.

Beloveds, limitation gives the meaning of growth.

You have come to know what it is to fail, what it feels like to be hurt, what it feels like to experience loss. We tell you that you have examined, probed at all the aspects of a denser reality, and now it is for you to come and experience, experiment with the lighter frequencies of light.

For truly, your liberation is when you take flight. The lightness of your heart is all that is to be gained, for you have carried so much that kept you in shame or judgment. Now, the time has come when you can release and let go of all the pain and turn it into something you have gained. Yes, you have gained knowledge, but now the heart can transform it into wisdom, to be the master co-creator of your life.

For all your limitations are here to bring you a teaching, to assist you to figure out your humanness and evolve it into more light. It has always been written that your liberation would come. But you thought it was something out there instead of living right in there inside your very heart.

We come and celebrate with you that your discoveries can be undone, to experience more creations in the master of the heart. The many dimensions of light hold the consciousness of many aspects of you. Your consciousness is vast, for the universe and more contains you. Now, we say, awaken into the masterful self.

DISCIPLINE

For some, this word has a negative feeling. It is related to having something forced on you when you were a child at home or at school and to some extent, not being or not feeling free.

If you look closer, you will discover that discipline is needed to change negative habits or old patterns. So often, your subconscious chooses something that you know is not good for you, but you seem to not be able to do otherwise; this is when discipline is needed.

We are talking about the discipline that helps you thrive and achieve when your fears in the subconscious say otherwise. When you connect with this discipline, you connect to a potent energy, that comes to hold you, to help you stay focused on something important for you. It comes from deep within, when you know a change is needed, to help you move out of destructive behaviors.

Do not force the discipline upon you. Instead, merge and weave your feminine energies of nurturance and comfort within and through you to restore balance into your body and soul. We are asking you to perceive discipline as awareness rather than something you need to force, do, or control. Bring awareness to your masculine and feminine energies and allow the flow of creation to move with and through you.

Your subconscious mind that has beliefs that are not aligned with this new idea, this new way of living, can overpower your experience if it is not brought in your conscious awareness. When you become aware and understand that balance is needed, shifts occur.

Discipline or train your mind to focus on awareness. It is not used against you; it is to be used to help you change your destructive and limiting habits. This energy will then help you discipline yourself to open to change, to allow something new.

Often, when a new idea, crosses your mind, like a flash coming through, your cells shiver, as they know it to be the Truth. It is unusual, however it holds a profound knowingness in you, as you can identify this as your soul whispering something new or different. Nevertheless, when your habit is different, you will need the energy of discipline to focus on awareness and shift your energies into balance.

Disciplining yourself to choose through awareness is the key to your success. This will help you rebalance your body, mind, and spirit. It will help you succeed in unknown areas and open you to a new reality and life. It will help make sure you choose what is good for you and achieve your highest potential.

Can you soften into the beauty of you? Can you pause to remember the space of love within you?

Do not let the mind criticize. Instead allow the breath to bring you to the opening of life that waiting for you.

Do you have the willingness to see the beauty that you dream to be?

Do you have the strength of love to pour on through from above?

For when you do, the earth does embrace you and light codes of joy begin to fill you.

Beloveds, when you "think" that discipline is only for the mind, you will seek and seek until you find more of what you cannot find. Instead, the discipline on which the mind can focus on is simply awareness. Be aware and forgive the criticism that you hold upon yourself; for the ego likes to judge and hold you in contempt.

Instead, we say allow more ease into the mind and simply know that you are enough. Know that you have already been given the glory of this new insight.

MEDITATE ON YOUR INNER GIFTS

What are your inner gifts, do you ask? Your response will evolve, and suddenly something else will come to light. We ask you to see for yourself as all the gifts are held within you until they are ready to be discovered.

Each one of you is connected to the universal wisdom of all that is. Therefore, even if you might not know it, you already transmit wisdom; you channel information and are a being of light and love. We are here to support you to choose to transmit through words, writing, paintings, sounding, and any other means of expression. As you express your creative nodes of creation within you, you connect to your divine nature.

You are gifting and anchoring, co-creating with all of humanity a new collective experience as you have chosen to be incarnated on the earth at this time of the now. Connected with the beauty of nature, family, community, and intimate relationship, you are all seeding love and prosperity at another level that has not been achieved before on the earth.

Through your evolution, you are rediscovering the power of appreciation and gratitude, as all grows far beyond that which you can imagine. Humanity is learning how to release fear and judgment by opening to the consciousness of One that changes the paradigm from which you are creating. With the feeling of compassion and knowing that all is you, however way you choose to do this, you will uncover all that you are as you open your channel within and allow miracles to happen, opening the mystery of creation.

We ask you to meditate through stillness on what you are truly. Meditate through your inner heart on the gifts you come to offer for the seeding of a new human experience. What rejoices in your heart? What is important for your soul? Choose to disconnect from any distraction that does not allow you to take time to mediate within, as what you imagine today will be your tomorrow!

Beloveds feel the weight of your body on your chair. Feel the clothes on your skin. Take a deep breath, let out a sigh, a sigh for the day, a sigh for your thoughts, a sigh for the unknown. Feel the weight of your body on the ground. Feel your clothes on your skin. Let your hearing be wide and open without labeling what you hear. Taste. Smell. Feel the weight of your body on the chair.

Now imagine you are walking down a path during the day. It is a warm spring day when things are just starting to renew. Smell the new air. Feel the breeze against your skin. Notice the ground you are walking on. Notice the trees, birds, or any other blessing that is before you.

Notice the clouds floating by and feel the sun's warmth on your skin. You now come to a gateway of sorts. Maybe it is two trees with a canopy, two stone pillars, or a doorway of sorts. Whatever you can imagine, it is your gateway to a new beginning. Enter this place of peace and serenity. There are no worries or stresses. You are safe and held by all the abundance that surrounds you. Every living thing around you supports you, the wind, the birds, the grass, the flowers, the trees, the animals, and the nearby brook. All this and more supports you.

As you breathe, you take in more life force. It fills you and rejuvenates you, heals you, making you anew. Find a place to sit or lie down to relax, for you know another blessing is about to be bestowed upon you. Wait and watch for the blessing. Does it come through a person or loved one, an animal, an angel, your higher self, a guide, or a master?

Maybe it is a message upon a rock or a sign in lights. Whatever it is, watch and wait. Don't worry if it doesn't come right away. Maybe the blessing is a feeling of peace, of stillness and quiet. Do not force it. Just open to the mystery of the blessing and allow yourself to discover the unfolding of miracles as you relax every cell, as you relax your mind. Let your thoughts fall to no words. But just experience your senses, feeling the ground beneath you and your breath within you. Feel your belly rise and fall to the peace of the inhale and exhale.

Allow this place of wonder to hold you deeply within all the *is*-ness of no time. Now what is the blessing that is being bestowed? Sit and ponder this for a while. When you are done, bow in gratitude and embody this blessing through and through. Start to walk back along the path to the threshold you came through, taking the blessing with you and holding it in your heart.

Slowly walk back.

Feel the weight of your body. Feel your clothes on your skin. Let your hearing to be wide and open. Taste. Smell and slowly come back. Wiggle your toes and move your hands. Take a deep breath and smile. Open your eyes. Feel the peace, the serenity, and blessing within your whole being. It is yours and will always be for the asking. Know that you can come back to this place at any time.

This is your blessing place, your safety place, and place of bliss.

HOW CAN I BE OF SERVICE IN TIMES OF CRISIS?

Now it is time, time just for the now. It is not a time to think about the future. It will come, it will come to you, you will know. Now is the time for you to practice staying aligned, staying in higher vibrations, as it is a pivotal moment in the now. Slow down; introspection is requested, by staying in the now through higher vibrations with an open heart to you.

Increase the gratitude that you hold within and trust that spirit has a plan, as you already know nothing is ever wasted. Currently, it is a time of not knowing, not knowing what you will be doing, but anchoring the faith that all is taken care of. It is time for you to open, to commit to open your heart, to amplify love and gratitude in co-creation with spirit. Profoundly know that something waits for you, something new, it cannot be of the mind, for it is new.

It is for you to open your heart to the unknown. Spirit knows that you are in service, but your service right now is to stay in higher vibrations day and night, night, and day. Allow change to happen by connecting to the consciousness of all the other beings on this planet that are elevating their vibrations to seed the new. Commit to release the old and birth the new.

It is certain from a human perspective, you cannot even imagine what will unfold, but you have a higher consciousness that has already achieved awakening and enlightenment, as you are truly already a pure divine being of love.

It is through the power of gratitude, love of self, that you will open to who you really are. All your gifts are already present; there is nothing you need to do, to learn. It is through the allowing, the opening of your heart to yourself, staying in higher vibrations, releasing the old habit of living, and sitting disconnected in lower vibrations that you take the time to reconnect to the beauty of the heart within. So, know you are given time and in this time; it is for you to connect with all the beings around the world that are elevating their vibration, their consciousness to seed the new. Be assured and reassured, that all is taken care of, that your call to service is understood and heard. You will be guided to fulfill your mission and purpose.

But for the present of the now, it is through your choice of vibrating a higher consciousness, preparing your body to anchor more light through the opening of the heart to the power of love, by doing this you already are fulfilling your mission and purpose of the time now.

Have faith! And know that all is taken care of. We wish to thank you for this service of the now, that together you will seed heaven on earth. Let the beauty be you, let the magic speak through you. Beauty you are, beauty you will be, and beauty all around you. Let the magic move through and create the beauty too, as you walk upon the earth creating something new. Everyone brings his or her higher light, building a master code as together you will know and expand into something new. Together, you will fill a new day that will dawn the unity of One.

Birthing the new
Birthing a new
Birthing, birthing
Breathing the new
We love you,
We honor your service,
Be the master that you are.
Share the light that you are.

SURRENDER—Pray More Plan Less

The purpose of this code is to remove the barriers and blocks that keep you separated from your ancestors, the lineage of which you were born. This will allow you to accept and honor the learning that each member of your clan has offered to the family. This code activates your willingness to release judgment and resentments that you may hold and allowing you to surrender to the teaching that each soul is bringing to you.

We understand that this is often difficult and may seem impossible, but we encourage you to open to the possibility that all has a purpose and that each soul that you encounter can bring you an awareness that you are holding onto density that no longer serves you. The karma that has been created can be transformed for yourself, others, your entire family, and ultimately for the collective of humanity. Imagine this code spinning through your energy field and all your systems, chakras, and energy bodies; this works just with your asking. Allow it to clear and release any blockages and attachments that hold you in separation, attached through your ego, mind, and spirit. With only your intention and willingness, it can soften you and allow room for more space within, offering a more peaceful experience.

CHAPTER 2
SURRENDER PRAY MORE, PLAN LESS

It is time to allow your thoughts of doubt to melt away. Breathe into the present moment. Your energetic frequency and vibration will rise as you focus on awareness. Stop the worry and release the need to know and allow the plan to unfold. You are to practice being present in each step of the way. This mastery will take intention and diligence to successfully maneuver through the unknown.

You are to bring sacred intention into your life. This is the prayer. The prayer is not something that you say, but rather something that you choose. The prayer is integrating structure and form into higher vibrational light from conscious co-creation. This is how you will birth a new world. When you use your life force with intention, you become the living prayer.

You realize that you can release control and that you do not need to know the whole plan—only move with consciousness each step of the way. You understand that you are only required to make conscious choices when needed and that, once you choose, you can always choose again as you hone your craft of conscious co-creation.

As you focus on what you want to create, the universe puts people and situations in front of you giving you opportunities to choose and consciously co-create. Instead of living a life haphazardly, you live a life as a ceremony fulfilling your soul's mission and purpose on the earth. The sacredness of the everyday is brought to the fullness of life, as moments are cultivated through higher awareness and nurtured through the gateway of the heart.

Open now and receive this grace to move with confidence that the past is now done, and a new beginning is here.

Be the prayer. Pray more. Plan Less.

INNOCENCE

SURRENDERING TO GROWTH

Living with consciousness in every moment is precious; it is the one and only chance in that instant.

When you live through the ego's need to protect and survive, you often create a hectic life. You barely have time to breathe. You go from thinking to doing, to doing to thinking. This infernal cycle distances you from experiencing the instant of infinite and limitless blessings.

We are here to remind you that the abundant nature of the universe is all around you. There is nothing lacking. It is only your perception that tells it is so. Focus on awareness. Love and calm your ego, as if it were a child. Tell it that all will be well. You are no longer trapped in the unconscious behaviors of rushing to and fro. Instead, you are aware, and your heart is connected to the unending flow of miracles, for a miracle is a shift in perception. You now see anew, for the miracle is you.

When you wake and say, "Good morning life! What miracle do you have for me today?" You start living in wonder that opens you up to all possibilities. Your mood is lighter. You start giving freely without waiting for anything in return. You experience moments of bliss and are fueled to discover more. You are grateful and lovingly accept all that is before you because you know you have the power to shift and create miracles once more.

As a conscious co-creator, your vibration increases, it becomes so much simpler to be. By smiling at what you call your imperfections, you can do so with glee. By loving deeply your body, this physical self that you see, you transform your manifestations to allow spirit to bring forth the keys, the keys to opening to your precious gifts that can be birthed within a moment of endless possibilities.

When you step out of the judgment on how things should or should not be, you can live a new experience without attachments or expectation and still, your dreams, powerful in their essence, pulse forward. You can feel the fire burning inside of you. You feel alive and full of passion and profoundly trust that life is taking care of you, not knowing in your mind what is going to happen, but with the wisdom of the heart. As a conscious co-creator, you are equipped with all you need as you enter the mystery of creation where all is possible way beyond your imagination.

Love is a byproduct of this way of being. Romantic love is no longer the goal, being conditional on another rather than loving no matter what the condition. Love is a state of being and the conscious co-creator embodies love as a sovereign being co-creating with the higher echelons of light and the world around them. The co-creator enters the realm of limitless potentiality because inner wisdom is then the guide to making conscious choices as you relax the mind and connect through the heart. You merge the peace of the heart with the focus of the mind and then you may act, choose, and co-create.

If your mind questions and struggles to find an answer, know it is not the way of the heart and start the process: radiate love, listen to the wisdom of the heart, find the peace, and then focus the mind to act.

These experiences provide the greatest potential of growth for you and those around you. When breaking a pattern and choosing differently than you have before, it may be uncomfortable for you and for others. Remember, a new spiral is becoming, growing, and expanding as the evolutionary process continues. Conscious co-creation is being birthed; be gentle with yourself and others as you practice and master the art.

The conscious co-creator has faith in their abilities and in their life. They remind themselves that all is moving in a cycle, spiral of evolution, ascending and descending, growing and retracting, offering fluidity and contraction. Sometimes life seems to be easy and sometimes it is so difficult, this comes from the spiral of life. When life becomes uncomfortable and sometimes painful, it is simply because you are in the cycle of the expansion of consciousness. Transform your limitations and grow. When life is easy, you are in a phase of integration and anchoring all that you have learned. These two go together, they are nonnegotiable, after the rain there is sun.

INNOCENT CHILD WITHIN

Run through time and
Return to the purity within
Dance through the rain with joy and
Return to your innocence
Come to this sacred space
Where all is yet to be discovered
As you are welcomed by the child
Who joyfully waits for you?
Reclaim your magnificence
Retrieve your beauty
In this space of wonder,
Where all is seen with awe
Allow yourself to discover
The sacred gardens that surround this innocence
This precious part of your soul
Untouched by the burdens of the experience
Feel the wind blowing away all your misery
Allow the waters to wash away all your sorrow
Enable the earth to hold you deeply
As you connect through these sacred gardens
As the child takes you by the hand,
Guiding you through the wind of change
Jump into the unknown
Allow your heart to expand
As you receive the love of your sacred child within
Do not take things so seriously
A smile can change your day
Open your eyes to see the beauty that surrounds you
Remember that you are never alone
That this precious innocence is you
Retrieve your child within

Allowing you to move through life with an open heart
As the gift of grace pours through this gateway
Allow yourself to giggle for you to share joy
Show all around you the pure love that you are
No need to be frightened of being hurt through
your vulnerability
As your given nature is untouchable
And you are pure love in essence
Discover the world through new eyes
Choose to see love and share your joy
And remember the innocent child lies within

EMOTIONAL TRAUMATIC MEMORIES OF CHILDHOOD

We wish to share that this wounded part of self will need love and kindness, as it triggers the way you react to what others say or what life brings your way.

It is important for you to understand why these wounds of your inner child are so profoundly invisible, and why you sometimes create so much drama through this conditioning. The child until five or six years old cannot rationalize, as the neo-cortex brain has not yet developed. That means that the child only experiences through their feelings and interprets the situation, perceiving itself as the center of it all. When the child experiences trauma, fear, or negative feelings, they will assume that the cause was their fault, even if it has nothing to do with them.

Like computers, children store data from their childhood within their subconscious. Through the energy of chaos shared by their parents, a feeling of doing wrong and sometimes even guilt may be imprinted within them.

This distortion creates misunderstanding and carries over into adulthood.

As an adult, your thoughts and feelings of trauma and limitations continue to be recreated in your life's experiences. Your wounded inner child will be lashing out and calling to you to be heard, as you will be creating from this place of feeling each time you react to any situation. Sometimes, you will even wonder why you reacted in such a way, as if someone else had taken over you, creating so much pain and suffering.

Your inner child holds emotional traumatic memories that were transferred to the subconscious so that they could move on. They hold many memories of abuse of all sorts, as they are birthed through innocence. This creates major distortions, perceiving all through limitations. That is why it is crucial to take time to connect with your inner child, to listen to what they have to say, and for them to realize that they are in no way responsible. When you do this, you allow the healing, transformation, and transcendence to happen through the power of love, compassion, and infinite kindness.

This will disable your conditioned reactions, allowing a more peaceful and loving experience with all that is around you. Conscious co-creation can transform and heal childhood wounds by bringing awareness to the honoring and acknowledging of the inner child. The original innocence of the child is restored and brought back into harmony and balance of your being.

Beloveds, all you need to do is *be*, be authentically you. The child wants to live without judgment and blame. Do not let your mind be the dictator of your actions. Instead, let the heart lead the way. Let your authenticity arise from the innocence of love, the original blueprint of you. The child's gift is that of the heart as it grows and discovers. The child is open to wonder, but when it is scolded or hurt, the feelings are great within. It is the cycle of transformation for every soul to know more of itself. For what is growth if you always know? Allow the cycles of co-creation to birth of a new day. Allow the cycles of co-creation to bring you away from the past and the future too, because everything can be transformed by you.

In the moment of the now, you can access your feelings of what you have buried and chose to not look upon. Come and discover the child that is hidden within you. The conscious co-creator is ready to be birthed within you because he or she knows that her child of innocence is there to assist you. Everything can be merged in the purity of heart, where everything can be restored rather than severed apart. What was and what ever shall be is the discovery of your innocence of thee.

LIVING IN HUMILITY

FEAR

We would like to talk about fear and how it is hidden in your everyday existence. It is camouflaged in many thought patterns. You do not realize that these thought patterns have held you back for so long because you have accepted this as your truth. But we say, that for you to know the fear, you are to recognize the very core issue of what you resist.

This is where trust and action are to be the dance. Since fear is hidden and you often do not like to see it, feel it, name it, nor claim it, it continues to be masked in many thought forms. Your fears are married in belief systems regarding your obligations, responsibilities, willfulness, attachment, or whatever your mind will rationalize is the right thing to do.

Beloveds take hold of the unknown. Within this place lies the liberation that you seek. Your freedom prevails when you are willing to move through the fear of the unknown. The mind tries to make sense of it all. The mind will come up with many plans, but we say, choose with peace. Use the fuel of the fear and transform and allow the space for love to dwell within the heart instead of judgment and pain.

Allow the winds of change to move with you, to support the cycle of growth that is waiting to be birthed into a new conscious creation. Soften the grip and let go of the need to know, to control and act with the willingness to see a new way. Take joy in the unknown and release the need to judge. You get stuck because you are afraid of what will be. Instead, we say, choose the choice that brings you to the balance that you seek, and all will align within thee.

Notice when fear arises, your mind starts swirling around and your imagination of the potential's threats start to fill you up. This can create chaos in your body, slowing down all your functions, you cannot think properly, you cannot see any positive issue and the decisions you take are based on the possible lack of something, so very often you inevitably regret them.

So, when fear tetanizes your body, STOP and BREATH in deeply! You have the choice to either stay in the fear or access your conscious co-creative power to step out of the illusion as most of the time you are not in real danger. So, take the time to just stop whatever you are doing, when this is possible, and breathe deeply; wiggle your body to shake off the fear. Choose to step out of this overwhelming feeling that does not serve you and reconnect to the present moment, freeing yourself from the illusion of this fear.

Once you breathe and shake your body to release the fear that was starting to overtake your power, you start becoming a true actor of your experience. You allow yourself to become the conscious co-creator of your experience in this moment, by not allowing the memories of the past to become the reality of the present. Fear is always based on the reactivation of a feeling of disempowerment of the past, when you thought you were the victim of life and others.

You are not a victim and never have been. You are a powerful co-creator of your present moment, and if you choose to let the past emotions overwhelm you again, you will be living the exact same experience over and over again, making it not only one experience but a belief where you might even think that you are cursed and not powerful.

You have no action on what experience comes your way, what happens is the doing of life. Where you do have the power is on how you experience what comes to you. When you realize what frightens you, you can decide to step out. You will realize that this is not true; it is only your mind that is projecting the past on the future and creating chaos in the now.

Beloved Ones, if you are not in real danger in the now, please choose to step out of the untruth of the fear and say three times, out loud if you can, *"NO, this is the past projecting on the future, it is NOT true, and I choose to stop this destructive behavior that does not serve me in this present moment; I am safe and taken care of."*

Then STOP and breathe; take the time to breathe in the support of Mother Earth and her blessings. This powerful being of creation is always surrounding you to support your growth. You co-create with her even if this is unconsciously. Through the law of attraction, she brings to you what your energy is calling for, so release the fear as it will create more fear. Allow yourself to feel her support; open your heart to welcome her in your life. Call in her support in all that you dream to create. The more it is for the good of all, the more power she will place in it.

Beloved Ones, allow yourself to be bathed in her arms, knowing that she is making all things happen, and that if something comes up that is not easy to live, it is a teaching for you, it is a gift that will help you release old patterns of conditioning so that you may create hand in hand through the power of love and for the good of all. Then you may also call in the power of the sun to bring you strength and clarity of the mind. Allow its rays to warm you and enlighten you, burning alchemically all that can be released, enabling the assistance of unseen realms to pour into your life to illuminate your path.

Stop the mind's patterns and breathe into the energy of balance. Feel the vibration of the enlightened way. Feel it through your heart center. Know that you are guided when you maneuver through the heart. It will lead the way. The mind focuses on the action, which consciously co-creates the birthing of anew.

The new is restored once again within you. Round and round we go. Creating a life you have never known, but wished and dreamed for within the nodes. May you be blessed as you release the illusion of fear!

WHAT IS THE PATH OF HUMILITY?

The gift of humility is the knowing that there are things that you do not know. It is releasing the need to understand and to control the situation. It is focusing on awareness and realizing that you are not the mind. The conscious co-creator stays in the humility of his or her own integrity and no longer has the need to prove themselves right. The conscious co-creator steps out of the construct of the ego and focuses on their very light, their creative power.

This blissful path is the opening to a new world, that in which you are free of the mind and you can follow the guidance and inner wisdom. It is the release of the need to be better than another, and the need of proving that you are different, as indeed you are unique, however as important as another.

When living this path, you grow into more of your uniqueness, you cherish yourself, and you allow your light and love to ignite. You profoundly know that you are the magnetic star that you are, and you no longer need to make sure that you exist.

The path of humility will take you deep within and you will discover all that you thought that you were not, all that you thought you needed to create. You will discover the bliss that lives within and profoundly know that you are divine, that you are the gift. This will then allow you to share with all what you are here to offer, participating in the awakening of a new world where all will be shining their light so that together you can ignite a new co-creation.

In the process of the cycles of creation, the surrender to what you think you knew can often be challenged. We ask that you become flexible in your thoughts and thus your feelings can move throughout your being of what you think you are and what you think you are to stand for. For the energies will move round and round and you can allow these feelings to take you on a journey from confusion into peace. We ask you to notice and be aware of the cycle. Do not judge, just notice. As you allow your awareness to take precedence, you become the observer rather than the controller. When one tries to control, the resistance to its higher knowing of trust is lost. We ask you to drop into your heart and allow the breath to fill you.

In this place you come home to your sacred place within. You start to realize all the blessings that are around you. You bow in gratitude and expand more love in your heart. Wisdom is the knowing that you do not need to control nor know all that will unfold in the moments. Wisdom is the knowing that you are equipped to withstand all that comes before you. Humility allows the wisdom to be part of the experience of this newfound you. For humility is part of the transformational process from one pattern into another. So, allow the violet light to churn and churn as humility transforms the old into new form.

FORGIVENESS

It is possible to for-give; however, this is a process. It cannot be rushed. Forgiveness is not only of the mind, but the heart. If you only process forgiveness in the mind, your cells would not feel it and it would not be complete. Sometimes it takes more time than others, as you are in resistance to what happened or to the pain and the suffering that is associated with this experience.

It is through the willingness to forgive that you will find peace in due time. However, focusing on this by repeating that "I am willing to forgive…" you instruct spirit that it is time for you to move on. Nevertheless, you will need to surrender to how this will happen and when you will be completely in peace with another and yourself.

Within this process, you start to forgive the other for all the harm that they may have caused. Ultimately, you travel around the spiral again with the awareness that what is required is to forgive yourself for having let the other person abuse you in any way. You then promise to love, honor, and respect yourself fully from now on.

It is through gratitude from within your heart that you will learn that all has come to you for a reason and that everything has a teaching. All the information that you gather through your experiences, all that shows up in your life, has a sole and unique purpose that contributes to your evolution. Your experience with others helped you regain what you thought you lacked but was only hidden in the temple of your heart. These life experiences provided you with the opportunity to love yourself so that you may honor your authentic self and share your gifts. You are given the opportunity to become more conscious, more loving. You are on the path of being a conscious co-creator.

Beloveds, in your pain, you may lash out at others. You may feel slighted, ignored of not being treated fairly. When this pain comes up, you find yourself more negative. However, the potential for the opening of your heart is great. Here in the eye of the storm of your own thoughts and grief lies an opening for a release. For when you bring consciousness to the pain, you are opening to the mystery within. You do not need to know how to forgive. All you need to do is to consciously open your heart by focusing on your heart center and breathe with the intention of opening to the grace of love, that is all. Take this time to allow the gentleness of love to pour through you. Relax into the deepness of the Earth Mother's heart as you ground into the center of your being and feel the connection. Breathe.

Forgiveness is not of the mind. It comes from the heart first and then the mind can align with the peace of your heart. Take the time to exercise the opening and expanding of your heart center. In the subtleness of love, it will come.

DIVINE

IN TRUTH, YOU RECEIVE ALL YOU NEED

The truth that you have all that you need is somewhat difficult to understand and anchor within self as you are conditioned through the collective consciousness with beliefs and programs of lack.

In the present moment, all is given to you when you are fully connected and aware. When you live from experiences of your past or project into the future, your being shifts from being whole to becoming limited and disconnected. It is through the now moment that abundance is accessed. The journey of the soul is to live in the presence of its true light and unlimited potential. The experiences on the earth give you many opportunities for the soul to journey through density and arise into more growth.

To release the past, take a moment and go back to a time in your life where you were a child and experienced some trauma. You may have most certainly worked on this issue numerous times, and still it never really dissolved for aspects of the pain still exist within you. No matter how much you have accepted, forgiven and loved this part of your young age, time seems blocked, and you cannot access the time before the trauma existed. Take time to go back to that incident and write down all that arises. Write down your thoughts and feelings, releasing all that is stored in your physical body.

Then, when nothing more comes to you, start to ponder what your experience was like before the painful incident occurred. Go back to an experience when all was well and you were able to be your authentic self in a space of innocence and love. Write down all that comes to you. Take time to feel it, sense it, and enliven it again.

Allow this memory to fill you and integrate into your experience of now. Unify your *beingness*. Allow this experience to become your new starting point, your point of reference. Be, feel, and sense this new truth and rewrite this truth on the timeline of your life, year after year, moving it forward and allowing yourself to experience a profound changing in the body and bring it back to the present moment of the now.

The collective consciousness of humanity is learning to journey through the process of releasing the illusion of lack, fear, and separation to recall its true nature, evolve, and enlighten. All that is proposed on a collective and personal level, has only One intention, to allow each and everybody to step out of their limited beliefs, to release pain and suffering, and reconnect to the wisdom within, which is only pure consciousness, bringing joy, peace, and fulfillment for all.

YOU ARE A LIVING TEMPLE

You are a living temple in divine perfection. All that is asked of you is to experience it, as you do not need to activate or energize it. You are to live it consciously as you co-create the life you dream.

When you walk in this knowing, there is no need to preach nor be dependent on another. You live limitlessly by simply being present. Everything around you responds and reverberates in this new awareness because you become a beacon of light that illuminates the path ahead. Instead of sitting in the shadow, you seek and become the power of transformation through love, and you begin to live a life fulfilling your purpose.

The temple is within you. When you look to the outside world to fulfill you, you will not find the peace that you crave. The peace and harmony that you seek can only be created within. The conscious co-creator cultivates the living temple within and embodies this energetic light. In this resonance, a new world can be seen, formed, and experienced. When things are chaotic or dissonant, the conscious co-creator comes into stillness. In the stillness lies the jewel waiting to be discovered within the center of the heart. The pressures of the ego provide many opportunities for the conscious co-creator to shine their diamond light.

The peace and harmony within create a masterpiece of love, which is you, Beloveds. It is you. It has always been you. The light and love that you seek is within you. No other person or thing can give this to you. You are the living temple. The more you go to the temple within, the more your frequency and vibration starts to resonate your soul's higher call.

Do not be a stranger to you. Know thyself and all will be given in the light and love of all there is. Know thyself and feel the freedom that is held from the strength of love you have built within yourself. You hold the keys to your deliverance. You create the breath of intuition and magnification within the living temple and life supports the living of your unique gifts, your individual code essence.

Be life, Beloveds. Be love. Be the Living Light Temple and behold the Flame for All.

ASKING YOURSELF QUESTIONS

It is time to seek the guidance within instead of seeking the answers from others. The process of integrating all parts of you will allow the wisdom to arise in your awareness.

Start from this place of consciousness, and remember that you are already there, you are already divine in nature and you have nothing to look for as nothing resides outside of you. Let yourself sit in the beauty of your divine nature.

Becoming the master is to start asking yourself questions, to hear the guidance you receive within without having to listen to what others have to say.

We wish you to take time to consider answering a few questions:

- Do you have unlimited trust in the benevolence of the Universe? If not, why? Does this serve you to think this? If not, do you wish to change it?

- Do you have an unwavering trust in yourself? If not, why? Does this serve you to think this? If not, do you wish to change it?

- How will you know when you have reached a level of mastery of your own human experience?

Your answers will be your truth in this present moment, and this creates the perception from which you are creating your reality in the now. Contemplating these questions will allow you to transform to have more serving beliefs, so that you can explore new experiences. This is an ongoing process; you will be finetuning it. Slowly and surely, you will start choosing from a more conscious place, allowing more grace and ease to enter your daily life.

While entering your mastery, you will be able to feel good no matter what happens. Through this complete trust, you will be opened to receive. You will be living in the flow and experience more love, peace, feeling blissed and whole. You will stand in your sovereignty and in your power as a vessel of conscious co-creation. By anchoring unlimited trust, you are aware that all your life experiences are here to support and guide you to live your highest potential. You are confident in this knowing and you exude this confidence to those around you.

Beloveds, when you perceive your life in wonder and in curiosity, you allow your mind and body to open to new possibilities. If you allow pure curiosity to energize any question, you will be guided and pulsed to explore. The pulse to explore brings you into the flow of the mystery. You are able then to maneuver on the waves of light that are beyond your human sight.

As you practice opening to the question, relax your mind. You do not need to rush around and find the answer to appease your fear, for that is not the intention. The intention is to allow you to wonder and to ponder to be in a state of exploration and discovery. In this state, you allow the mind to relax and the wisdom to arise, for the heart does know the whispers of the soul. Release this need and the struggle to know for this blocks the flow of conscious co-creation. Allow the flow and let it go as you travel on streams of consciousness that are clear, precise, and sublime.

TRUST

TRUSTING THE UNIVERSE COMES TO ULTIMATELY TRUSTING YOURSELF

When you do not trust, you do not allow the energy to come through, you enter a control mode, you do not receive any guidance, and life becomes a real struggle. You enter denser states of consciousness, living in fear, pain, and suffering as you create a lot of drama around you.

You are not the lack you experience. You are not the judgment you experience. It is only a creation that you believe to be true simply because you are used to living in the lower vibrations of doubt and fear. You replay this over and over and you call this your existence, your reality.

Beloveds, you can be the conscious co-creator now. Remember that you are created through higher vibrational light and you can use your energy with intention to live in peace, joy, abundance on all levels, harmony, and so much more.

When you are fully present in the moment, fully conscious, connected with everything around you, trusting that the energy of the Universe is here to serve you, you are then fully in your creative power. The intelligence that creates the world is not only out there, but it is in you too, and it is from within that you create your life experience.

If you can trust that you can stay present in the higher dimensions of consciousness, you will experience less struggle and suffering, as these are the experience of lower vibrations only. This does not even exist in the higher dimensions, as the purpose of the experience is another. And yet, you have come to experience the human experience. You are to discover and experience unity by moving in and out of balance. As you move through this energy, you will entrain into the unified field of oneness and become the crystalline blueprint of love.

Stay present and conscious in the very moment, trusting yourself and opening to flow of energy to run through you. Trust yourself, you are where you are supposed to be as you practice knowing your state of consciousness. Find a signal to remind your body and your mind to be conscious and receptive to the miracles of life all around you by opening and allowing energy to serve you in the highest way. You embody and trust the limitless benevolence of Universe.

As you fortify trust, you will come in and out of these vibrations. Lower vibrations, higher vibrations—all are a dance within the universe, as it is within. Do not judge yourself or criticize when you drop into lower vibrations and frequencies of lack and fear. You will continue to dance between the two to find out more of the self. You will be aware of all that you have created and experienced. You will tune into the streams of consciousness that were dormant before as you awaken more of your gifts and merge and marry other parts of your consciousness into the zero-point field of the eternal now.

When you are aware and conscious of the eternal moment, you allow trust to be you. For in this place of the eternal now, there is nothing lacking because you have accessed peace and serenity. Trust that you are made up of the universe and the universe is you. Your inner world reflects to your outer world.

Trust that if you are willing to see the beauty emerge within the darkness, then it will be. The light that breaks through the veil of fear is the light that is held in the clear, as the crystalline structure of your very veins starts to evolve into a new pattern again. Choose to trust the universe that works and lives in you.

OVERCOMING DOUBT

Beloved Ones, when you tap into the unknown, fear comes up. Do not try to make it go nor act as if it were not there. It is a natural process when birthing the new. It is merely something you have not yet experienced.

So, breathe, Beloved One, breathe, and allow the part of you that is in fear to come forth. Face it, because when you do, you start to release the emotions that overwhelm you. This is the first step in resolving what is getting in the way of your new creation.

Call in the breath of life, breathing in and out consciously. Center your mind and focus on the breath. Breathe in the love of life. Breathe out all that does not serve you, all the hurts you all that limits or contracts your body. Open now to a new possibility. When you breathe in, take in all the love we hold for you, as we are the Council of creation consciousness who assists you to birth the new. Connect with us now. Breathe in our assistance. Call on us as we surround you and embrace you with love. All you need is the willingness to let go and enter something new.

Breathe in and start to focus slowly on your belly, the region of your physical self. This is the place where there may be restriction, for within this energy center lays the fear of the unknown. Remember, it is natural for fear to arise when one is birthing something new. It is not to be denied, nor pushed away, as it will stay in the dark until you take time to embrace it completely.

The presence of fear may not be apparent. It will seem as if it does not exist. Yet, your soul patiently waits until you overcome this illusion and you are ready to face it. In the meantime, blocks are presented, and your creation is slow instead of in the flow, making the anchoring of your creation complicated.

Beloved Ones, consciously connect with the part of you that holds fear even if you do not feel it or sense it. At times, the fear may be buried so deeply that you have become numb to it. You dismiss it, saying it is not there because to look at it, to feel it, is the very thing that you resist.

We invite you, Beloved Ones, to sit back and breathe into the region of your belly, allowing divine love and compassion to enter the womb of your creation. Sit comfortably and allow the energies enter your body. Allow this region to expand. Allow the breath of life to bring in the energies of balance, so that the wind of love may enter through your breath and release all that you need to release.

This is a simple process that cannot be forced nor controlled. Allow the breath of love to overcome your fear and fill you with faith. Yes, the Universe has heard, Beloved, your heart dream. It is on its way. Do not doubt. You are worthy of living the life you dream and powerful enough to bring forth your gifts. Co-create with us and allow us to enter your world where all is welcomed according to the Law of One.

Stay consciously connected to the breath of life, the creation consciousness of one. Allow your fear to be shown to recognize, accept and come back into love for yourself. We remain at your service throughout all your creations.

SURRENDER IS THE FLOW

It is not always easy to surrender; it is a learning process. Train yourself to live the attitude of surrender, as it will bring harmony and strength into your life experiences.

Trust in the Divine to help you release the need to control. The need to control comes from fear and uncertainty. Bring in the awareness that you are safe and secure. Feel the support from Gaia and the benevolence of the universe. As you are fully grounded in this safety, you make it easier to let go and surrender. Do you believe that all is happening for you or to you? If you are not certain that all that happens in your life is going in the direction of more love, then we ask you to change your belief, choose to change now by opening to the possibility that the divine is working for you.

What is surrender? It is the ability to accept, without questioning what comes forth in your life, without wanting it to be otherwise. In challenging times, this is sometimes very difficult. Your emotions will need to be neutralized and balanced within you. Try not to control them or ignore them. Just notice that they are present. You do not need to become the emotion, only aware of it. The breath is a tool to bring in this awareness. Stay focused and ask for assistance from the Divine. As you do, you will allow your emotions to come to the surface to be expressed and released back into the ever-changing universe.

You are not your e-motions. Your emotions are energy in motion showing you where you are in any given moment. Think of emotions as your own internal GPS. It gives you the coordinates to where you are at any given moment. At the same time, know you can travel to another point when a new situation arises. The energy in motion is here to help you know and experience yourself fully. It is time to perceive it as a tool to become conscious and aware of what is going on inside of you.

Often, your emotions are not balanced because you either resist them or express them in pure reaction mode. We are asking you to perceive your emotions as a magical part of you that gives you signals and signs on your journey to awareness. Let your emotions become your friend instead of your enemy. Once you accept and understand them, you can neutralize them and choose from the alignment of both the heart and the mind.

Do not mistake your heart as your emotional center. Your heart is the gateway to the soul. Your emotions sit within other energy centers of your body. When you hold in, control, or ignore your emotions, you create a blockage to the energy that is designed to move and be in motion. This is the very resistance and tension you feel in your body. You feel stuck when the energy in motion is unable to move through you. Surrender is about consciously knowing when you need to allow the movement of your emotions to come through you. They will not stay if you allow them to move through as they were designed. You are then opened to receiving another experience as well as guidance from your internal compass because your energy system is flowing and circulating around you. Your senses enliven, your passion is stirred, and you are inspired to co-create with your soul.

If you do not allow the emotions to move through, your mind will start to go in all directions. It will want to take control. It will try to figure out a way to get out of a stressful situation. It will lament to understand what went wrong.

It will race to find a solution. You will be caught in a loop, a never-ending cycle of thinking and recreating the same stress and drama. Conscious co-creation is the journey of awareness that empowers your choices to choose from a place of stillness rather than stress or drama. When you honor your emotions and allow them to move through you, peace will naturally be restored within you.

By elevating your frequency and going within, you will access this harmonic place to hear the song of your soul to emerge. In this place, you allow surrender to be a conscious choice of empowerment rather than the decision to give up in shame and guilt.

Remember, throughout the process of conscious co-creation ask for assistance from the Divine, from your higher self, or from a loved one. Co-create an intimate relationship with Source and ask to receive the guidance and awareness so that your journey to wholeness is one of conscious choice and empowered love.

Beloveds, you are much more than you think you are. You have much more power than you believe. You are your body, and you are not, you are your thoughts, and you are not, and round and round the spiral will go until you understand that to know surrender is to be in the flow.

What is the gift? How will this go? Breathe into the light and watch the show. Realize the energies that move to and fro and understand that creation works best when you surrender to the flow.

THE CIRCLE—Starts with you

The heart is a portal through which you connect with all of creation. By breathing and opening your heart center, you will start to release the old stories that keep you in the illusion of separation. The purpose of this code is to allow you to know what it feels like to truly love yourself. In doing so, you reconnect to your true nature, the essence of creation from which you were born and to which you shall return.

Imagine bringing this code through your energy centers or chakras and through the multi-layers of your energy bodies that surround you. Allow yourself to open to all that you truly are as you place your intention in the center of your heart and breathe deeply. Feel the infinite love being poured through you and experience the power of this grace. Allow this sacred code to deeply open into your heart as you dissolve the blocks that keep you for opening more and more.

By releasing the barriers that guarded your heart for fear of being hurt, will now allow you to open to receive the love you have always desired. The journey of knowing the circle starts with you will help you release the illusion of separation and open you to receiving love and abundance on all levels.

CHAPTER 3

THE CIRCLE STARTS WITH YOU LOVE

LOVE

OPENING TO LOVING SELF

Are you ready to start loving yourself?

Are you ready to start to see the way that you are without judging yourself?

When you start opening your heart, you start opening your eyes and enter the temple of Truth. You start to see yourself clearly and see the limitations that you hold. These insights usually come through the challenges you face in life. These are the opportunities of change that life brings to you for you to understand who you are and what you can offer. By opening to the compassion of self and by loving yourself, you allow change to happen gracefully.

Can you allow yourself to feel love for yourself in this moment?

Can you allow yourself to hear and feel when you say to yourself "I love you," "I love you," "I love you"?

Take time to hold yourself in your arms and repeat again and again these magic words, "I love you." Speak them out loud so that you can hear yourself and physically feel it in the body. Feeling love for yourself, for your humanness will allow your brain to change its reality. This simple but powerful process will undo all the limitations you have built up over each time you judged yourself.

By taking a few moments every night and sharing your love with yourself, you release the stress. Your awareness and clarity will grow. This simple process anchors profoundly in your cells, the knowing that you are loved. When you love yourself, the depth of love you can share with another can also go deeper.

By doing this simple process every night before you go to sleep, your body will process and absorb this increase of vibration. You will familiarize yourself with these loving energies and integrate it throughout every part of your being. You will hardly notice it, but you will inevitably increase your vibration and change your life to experience more love.

This will open you to the new you, a more caring and loving you. This will change your perception and reality by offering yourself and others a more blissful life.

Traveling into the sun
is to walk through the majesty of you
Traveling into the sun
is the creation code of love
Let the song be given
Within your very core
Open and breathe now
And connect through your core
The mountains

And the trees now
Are your very friends,
The clouds now and the waters
Move through you too.
Life comes to you to change you
To remember the very code
That runs through you.
As your blood circulates
And moves through you
Allow the streams of light
To permeate through you
Feel the light
Breathe in the light
The magic is you.

When you get so tired of acting out of fear and control, you surrender and accept what you see. Feel your way through the pain, breathe into the rhythm, and know the direction of the soul. For the soul knows that you are divinity and worthy of love.

If only your ego mind can see the true blessings that have you on the go. Until another story comes its way through the dark and shadowy lands, you will try with all you might to make a stand and defend yourself instead of seeking to understand.

To understand your true nature is to simply be. In this state of being, love comes to your door asking to be invited in and be received. All you really need is the willingness to take heed and allow the opening of the heart to be the intention. Go beyond the parts of you that want to lash out in hate and instead open to your great fate.

Notice all the things you do without care for the self. Instead of being last, why not be first. All is served when one is fulfilled. There is no lacking and resentment to be because love is the giver for all who want to see. See yourself first and love yourself up because no matter what, it will always create your part. What energy do you want to create with, fear or love?

Let the transformation be in the moment of now. Open and embrace this now. Know that you are the star that you are— for everything within is coming from afar. The star needs to be known and to be discovered we say. So, bring love unto you on this day.

HEALING PROCESS

Transformation and healing take place when you allow judgment to drop and you release the need to punish another or yourself.

The healing process of transformation is one that allows the wholeness of your being to just be. If you heavily rely on the mind to know and understand "why" things happen, the more you will stay stuck in the past. The more you try to fix what has happened, the more you relive what you do not want. You are then caught up in a loop of distress and replay your fears over and over again. The more you "make sure that this doesn't happen again," the more you stay trapped in the illusion of fear.

In times of feeling pain, betrayal and abandonment say, *"I free my mind from trying to figure everything out. I will know when I need to know."* Stop the never-ending story of what was and live what is as a conscious co-creator of your life. Take back your power and arise into something more, becoming of the real you. We are here to remind you, Beloveds, you are more than you realize.

For if you really anchor the truth and empower your light, everything that comes to you will be what you have co-created in consciousness instead of living in the realms of the subconscious and unconscious fears of "what was" or "what could be." Instead, come into the healing power within that is devoid of judgment and comes from a state of pure love. In this state of willingness, by fully allowing and receiving energy, you open yourself to new possibilities where all can be restored and brought back to its purest source frequency.

Practice sitting. Love yourself by taking time every day to nurture your body. Allow love to emerge from the inside out. Bring the frequency of love to your physical body through the intention. Stay focused through the senses. Feel, smell, sense, and touch love. By staying in love with yourself, you allow love's high vibrations to balance, heal, and transform you to restore and rejuvenate every part of your being. Let the mystery of love be your experience. Manifest miracles and discover more of the unseen realms of a multidimensional conscious co-creator. Do this with the sole intention of bringing love to the self and all the rest will be taken care of.

But we say to you, as you awaken to your true light, you will understand that you can master your holy light. Just as in the days when miracles were told, so too can you be the master to behold. Miracles are within the realm of the beholder. You can mask away and turn away from the

light you hold, or you can transform and allow the miracle
to unfold.

Many Masters throughout time have given their stories.
They say in pure humility that you too can bring forth this
new way. When times are tough and you cry away your
sorrows, healing does come to shed light and transform for
a better tomorrow. The healing is your personal experience
of your holy sacred place. No matter what it seems to
others, you are the one to say what will be and will not be in
its place.

Come and discover the healing ability you can restore within
you and open to the magic and mystery that lies within.

CARING FOR OR CARRYING OTHERS

You are all on the path of evolution and learning to honor
and take care for the self is a very important part of it all.
What you cannot do for the self, you cannot do for another.
This is not from an egoistic point of view, obviously, but
from lovingness.

It is time for you to make the difference. Care for people
with infinite patience and love. Assist them to learn from
their experiences as you discover and learn from your
own lessons in care and in patience. As you empower,
you empower others. No need to have pity for others.
No need to save them too. Each soul pulses to find their
own journey of empowerment through consciousness, it
is not up to you. What is up to you is to do you. Find your
bliss, Beloveds that is all. Once you do, you heal, you can
then bless and contribute to a better world because you
simply are in it. Do not take the burden of another as you

carry your own. Transform what is within the depths of you. The journey is yours and it takes diligence and patience. When you transform your energy, your soul grows. This is the mission and purpose for the soul, to evolve and grow through consciousness. So, let go of the burden of trying to fix another, as it imposes your will upon them.

It is through your energy, words, love, and wisdom that you provide the tools or techniques to help others grow. It is through your *beingness* that you will radiate who you are, allowing others to be more of who they really are. Be the model of your own goodness.

When you feel the need to save or fix others, you carry the burden of illusion. It implies that you judge the other to be a victim and not being strong enough. You believe life to be unfair which holds the energy of judgment and deters you from healing, transformation, growth, and expansion. If you hold this judgment on another, you hold this upon yourself because you believe that you or another does not have the power to co-create a life they wish or dream of. All is only a projection onto another and instead of consciously co-creating with your higher light, you place a false sense of importance that tricks you into the illusion.

What you do in the name of love is instead an action of codependency. In codependency you rely on another to make you whole. You wait to be affirmed and validated to prove to yourself that you are worthy, or you project this belief on another. You have been convinced that you are not worthy. The long past wounds continue to play out until you say "stop" and you are ready to move and transform into something new.

When you fall into the pattern of fixing or saving another, you will realize that this is not effective for anyone. You are helping them stay the way they are because you do not give them the opportunity to understand how they are creating what they are living. Both of you are caught up in a cycle of recreating an old belief that you need to do something or be something to be loved. It may ease your ego for a while for you believe that doing for others because they cannot do for themselves implies that you know better and hold a sense of being better. This creates separation and instead of focusing on what you wish to co-create with others and your higher self, you are caught in the past replaying what you are trying to escape.

In all cases, notice this as a distraction, a habit, or a blockage for not fulfilling your purpose. Be aware. Are the choices that you make honor and support you? Beloveds, you have been taught that sacrifice is the great redeemer; that sacrifice will get you into the gates of heaven. But you have been taught through a perspective that sees you as a victim and not as the creator.

Sacrifice is to make something sacred. Sacrifice your need to prove you are good and instead come into your heart center and beam out your goodness. Sacrifice your need to let others know that you are worthy and instead hold compassion for others by allowing them to know that they are loved no matter what condition, and you will hold the vision for their highest good as well as for yourself.

Trust in your ability to create, Beloveds, and move out of victim consciousness and into creator consciousness. This is where the new world is seeded into being. This is the access point to birthing a new world.

SECURITY

You are a living light portal on the earth. Your body acts
as the main entry point for source energy to be channeled
to the earth and those around you. By living your gift
and becoming a conscious co-creator, you become the
expression of God eternal. Whatever name you want to call
it, you are source energy and you have been birthed from
this unlimited potential. Within the core of all creation is
love. The ability to access this state of consciousness is your
ability to understand all of who you are.

You are more than the body. You are more than your mind.
You are more than your emotions as there is so much more
to find. Allow the openness of love to be the discovery of
each day as you act as the gateway to creative potential
and put it on display. Share it with the world. Share it with
your friends. You do not need to have it all perfect, just be
in love with the play. Remember when you were younger
and you had fewer cares within your mind. Remember when
things were easier, and your imagination was your land. You
were able to create stories and instruments to bring into
your hands.

The most magnificent portal is the One of your heart,
though you may have been hurt and forgotten this mighty
light. You may have closed it and wished to never feel
any more fright. But we say to you that your heart is the
doorway that allows you to cherish yourself and another. It
is through the feeling that it can open again and rediscover.
But to do so, you need to choose to open your heart.
By living through the fear of being hurt, you dulled your
experience and disconnected from Source.

Whatever might have happened, it is time for you to step
out in full force. The force of love will bring you a new code.
That will awaken you as your bravery will take hold. As
you open to the change your life, you do so by choosing
to open to life. It is your essence and not something you
need to find. Open to love and let it transform all the pain
and allow the burdens to melt and be on its way. Allow the
expansion of your feeling, the expansion of love to be the
inspiration of change from the darkness into light. Allow
the intensity of the benevolence of life to come your way.
So, do not be shy, no need to be afraid. As the hard time is
of the past, as you have chosen to open your heart again.
Through the expansion of the love in your heart, you share
this vibration around you. You open to the fullest expression
of you. For you are love!

THROUGH ADVERSITY—HAVE FAITH

Faith is not a thing of the mind! When you feel discouraged,
stressed, or doubt the answer is faith. When you are
afraid of failure or feel unworthy, the answer is faith. Be
the witness of your life. Notice your anxiety and start the
process of retrieving the assistance of Spirit. The anxiety is
a symptom of feeling separated and alone and the mind
will race to make judgments and or solutions. The spiral
continues and around and around you go.

Beloveds, come out of the mind and into the heart of
faith. Withdraw from the spiral of anxiety and choose to
consciously open your heart. Allow the racing of your mind
to calm down and feel the rhythm of your body and breathe
the sacred breath as you enter in the fullness of the body.

By facing the fear or anxiety within, you courageously undo the habit of fleeing that is buried in your subconscious. This comes from ancient memories stored from situations were a matter of life and death fueled the collective consciousness of humanity with anger and fear. These memories are ingrained within you for you hold the memories of your energy and the collective, as all are One. Humanity's consciousness has evolved and so too you and still without awareness you will keep living the past memories of survival and pain even though you are not in danger of death you will continue to fear it for it is your instinct to do so. We say, Beloveds to come into awareness and co-create now with the Divine. Know that you are safe. Stop, breathe, and consciously open your heart.

Come into the present moment and consciously ask the mind to enter with you into the experience of the now. Choose to be in the current moment from a place of stillness and know that you will be able to confront whatever is before you because you are willing to transform into something new.

Slow down. Come into the sacredness of your being. Enter fully into your physical body. Feel, sense, know, and experience thoroughly through all your senses. Allow the breath of life to enter your experience. Allow the assistance of Spirit to enter your present moment.

Slowly, relax your body. Receive the support. We are sending you our loving embrace. Allow us to hold you in a field of oneness and stillness. You are safe and loved. Open your body and soften your body more and more with each breath. Relax your mind. Connect to your heart as all this love starts to circulate around you, infusing you with love and sharing all the goodness of life.

Breathe and open into the center of your body between your heart and your belly. Allow the breath of life to enter where your fears are stored. The sacred breath of love flows into the present moment. You are profoundly held, supported, and fulfilled.

Breath after breath, all comes back into divine order. The flow and connectivity of this miraculous energy rejuvenates within your body. Fulfillment and abundance are restored. You are anchoring, step by step, the profound sacredness that connects you to spirit.

By allowing spirit to enter your physical body, through the sacredness of the conscious breath, you receive the gift of faith. This gift is to be anchored again and again in the same way. Faith is not to be understood but rather experienced. The more you open to the experience of faith, the more you anchor it within your field of possibilities. Sense, feel, and know that you are not alone. You are worthy because you are in faith and you co-create with spirit. The entire Universe arranges itself around your dream as you live your gift and share it with the world.

THE DANCE OF POLARITIES

Your connection to spirit and your connection to the earth is your anchor point in this life. You are a bridge between heaven and earth. As you strengthen your field of light, you strengthen the bridge to harmonize the stars and the earth. The gifts from both planes come together to bring the gift of co-creation. The balance of feminine and masculine energies comes together to bring the gift of co-creation too. Beloveds, you are here to find the balance between the two polarities. This is the gift of your earthly plane. Your soul knew of the teaching of this plane. You have come to expand your consciousness and master co-creation in physical form, bridging spirit into form. The balance is found in the dance of life and in the flow of creation that is held in the state of love. This is the conscious co-creator's journey through life. It is infused with passion, creativity, and growth.

The true safety you seek will come from the practice of the dance of polarities. Observation without judgment gives balance to the polarities because you detach from the labels and are open and willing to discover something new. Be the scientist of your life and hypothesize. Be the experience of life as you imagine and co-create new inventions or structures. These units of co-creative work will be built upon a code that is fueled with unlimited source potential because it is fueled from the single point of ONE, not of judgment, but of love.

You have known the aspects of the polarities and have played them out collectively on your earth plane. You have experienced and witness the outcomes of the imbalance. Now, is time to unify, balance the heart and the mind, the feminine and masculine and the light and the dark. In the balance, you will become a unified field of light.

HARMONY OF THE HEART

POWER IS LOVE

When you are centered in your inner power, you feel at home. All is calm and peaceful.

The greatest strength is not through exerting power over another. It lies with the presence of your pure being. As you enter the stillness of yourself, the energies are soft and subtle. Yet, when experienced, there is nothing more vast and powerful. You enter in a non-force of infinite love. You are in communion with yourself and have access to all possibilities and to all creations.

This concept of power is so soft that it moves into every creation without any resistance. It opens all the doors to enable change at a very deep level. Humanity is still learning how to use this extremely powerful tool. This soft power is often perceived by the ego as scary because it feels vulnerable. When you look at a mother, she takes care of her child by nourishing and protecting it and her child cherishes the strength of her love. She is not weak. Her strength is in her vulnerability to love because she is open and willing to love her child without condition. A mother's belief in her child despite any mistakes and mishaps that are made is the strength of her love. She is vulnerable for she does not have control over every choice the child makes as they grow, but she knows her love for her child will never go. Her strength is her love. Her love is her strength. This is the truth of her power. This is the truth of love's power.

The source of this soft power is seeded in your consciousness. However, to access it, the conscious co-creator feels empowered within, connected, grounded, safe, and protected. The conscious co-creator engages with another through cooperation, negotiation, mutual respect, and compromise to reach solutions that satisfy both sides.

By centering your attention by relaxing in the breath, you open your heart to connect with the infinite power of love within. This infinite power is an inexhaustible source of creative benevolence because you enter the most transformative energy of LOVE.

Your creative strength lies in who you are, when you choose to awaken to the simple truth of your being. Enlighten your creations. Spread love all around you. Help create a better world.

CONSCIOUS RELATIONSHIPS

You are the lover, and you are the loved. Your relationship to yourself and your desire to explore your inner world is the energy you will put forth in your relationship with others. As you co-create with your higher light, you begin a relationship with the many facets of you. The first and foremost conscious relationship starts with you. Focusing on your presence will be the key to all your relationships. Therefore, we are here to bring you on the inward journey of discovery of the self.

As you begin this journey of conscious co-creation, you begin to balance within what was out of sync. We remind you to focus on your breath time and time again. Our intention is to bring you into the present moment. In this moment, nothing else exists. There is no past and there is no future. There is only NOW. The moment of NOW is the access point to your co-creation. Begin to create a conscious relationship with the moment of NOW.

We ask you now to consider all your ideas and constructs of what relationship is and simply put it aside. Consider these ideas and beliefs as limitations. Your thinking mind projects conclusions to a relationship that has yet to be experienced. You identify with these beliefs and limit your experiences. Instead of living a life that is fresh, spontaneous, and alive, you fill your life with ideas, constructs, judgments, conclusions, and outcomes. Thus, recreating more of what was then co-creating something magnificent, flowing, and new. Conscious relationships have a flow, an ease of relating because it is the intention to be present and aware.

To begin the process of conscious co-creation it is most effective if you let go of the whole idea of relationship all together. We ask you to focus instead on *just relating* in the present moment. It is an action of pure sensing that you can participate in the present moment.

Your conscious choice to live a more empowered life will reflect in your relationship with others. The level of intimacy that you crave will be discovered within. You will not be afraid to share with another the truth of which you are because you have already started to cultivate the relationship with yourself and you have drawn your attention back to the present moment.

The circle starts with you, Beloveds. No one can sustain the passion that is to move through you. This is the journey for each individual soul. You can rely on others to do this for you, and it will work for a while, but it will not sustain the passion within you because you are the only one who can fuel the energy of love and creativity that dwells deep within you. You are the creator of your universe and you project out as if it were on a movie screen the world that you perceive to see. Each and every soul's ability to respond to their soul's growth is the independent journey that contributes to the whole. The peace and harmony will come when people awaken to their gifts and masterfully co-create by relating instead of living in an old beliefs or conclusion that live in the ego mind.

Nothing is more important than conscious relationship. It is a basic and fundamental need for good health and fulfillment. However, when you play out through the ego wanting to win and prove that you are right, you expend much of your energy protecting the self instead of loving the self. Instead, the focus is on another to give you what you need which creates a lot of disappointment, frustration, and a sense of powerless. This belief is with the expectation of an outcome or conclusion. Love and your relationships will be based on conditions. The more conditions, the more trapped you feel. The more obligated you feel, the more you crave your freedom.

The ego uses various tactics as shouting, blame, self-pity, shutting down, or refusing to communicate. The old arguments keep on repeating themselves as each person is attached to his or her positions. This cycle will play out until one chooses to see another way and begins to take responsibility in co-creation.

If you could look at it from the outside without being triggered by your ego and emotions, you would see that this person with whom you have a conflict or argument with is triggering your past experiences. This construct or belief very often came from childhood. From early on, this belief was created and formed a habit, construct, or idea and started an action-reaction process that most probably did not serve you, and never will. The pattern played out unconsciously without awareness.

When you experience unresolved emotions when relating with someone by either in the way they acted or in what they said, notice how you feel. Do you want to immediately react, defend, or lash out? If so, you know that a memory is coming up to the surface. STOP in that moment and focus on awareness and be present. Step out of the unconscious behavior, breathe, and align to the truth of who you really are as a divine being of magnificent light.

If you forget and notice after the reaction, be gentle with yourself and know that you will have another opportunity to practice presence. Beloveds, you have experienced the outcome of your patterns for the old way of behaving will come up time and time again as you will repeat the same argument or experience the condition in the same way as in the past.

The friction you experience in all relations sheds a light on where you hold resistance. To look within takes courage, but we tell you that once you shine the light of what you did not want to see, you will then be able to create from your divinity. Acceptance is key. Your past experiences are here to bring you the wisdom to discover who you are. It is not to punish or limit you in any way. Stay present in the moment. All is given in the moment if only you wish to see, breathe, and sense. Bring conscious love and attention to heal.

In unconscious relations, every party thinks they are doing more than the other. Each individual feels that they are in the right and are justified. The ego is set up to protect and will defend at all costs. This is unconscious behavior from wounding of past experiences.

Having a conscious relationship does not mean that you have a calm and peaceful relationship all the time. It means that you are willing to bring awareness to your situations. Take time to reflect and go inside to see the part of you that is being triggered. Go back if necessary, to your Beloved and express how you felt. Do this without placing any guilt on the other. Simply share your feelings and how you perceived it to be. Be open to a discussion with the intention to seek clarity instead of projecting shame. In this conscious co-creation discussion, you will receive new insights about your true feelings and transform the pain by bringing to the light what was buried deep in the dark. Co-create a solution that brings in love instead of division. Be gentle and honest within this process of discovering the self. The Beloved you are relating with is your pathway to finding out more about yourself. When you are willing to experience something more, your choices will reflect that decision. Your decision will not come out of anger, but out of awareness and peace because you soul is pulsing to bring in harmony and you balance your heart and mind as One. As you do this for you, you allow the other to do the same for it is an individual journey into the self. Loving relationships are not a given; they require continuous attention as they reveal the areas where you need to grow.

By choosing to live in the present moment, you have the power to remain true to yourself and learn how to make healthy choices in all your relationship. From this conscious and loving place, you will easily give of yourself to others without forgetting yourself. Generosity and understanding will flow freely to all you care for. You will be in the flow of relating in the moment. It will be fresh, new, and alive.

You will see the others with new eyes because you will see yourself new. You will love yourself without a condition, as you will love others without conditions too. You will show kindness and have compassion because in essence you are saying, "Come passion let me witness you. Com-passion let me be a channel for you."

LIVING MORE OF WHO YOU ARE

Through the quantum field, you have access to all. Through the deep breathing and relaxing, you create a coherent field of oneness from which you can access to so much more.

May you come to know yourself, so that you may become more aware of whom you really are, expressing more of your divine truth.

You are greatly loved by all the beings that sit in the quantum field and all are inviting you to love yourself greatly. In the energies of infinite love, each one of you is a unique expression of the infinite universe. All that is taking place for you is in accordance with your unique universal wisdom, for you to remember the combination of energies that create your uniqueness, while being united with all.

Currently, the energy of the planet is increasing and inviting you to be more complete in every level of your DNA. This will enable you to radiate in all directions and send out the frequencies of infinite love. Through your inner alignment, you can express your wholehearted divine self and be all that you have come to be. You are united to the earth and to the sun, infinite love and universal presence opening through all levels of consciousness.

Observe how you feel, now that all has been said. Become more present in the now. Be ready to amaze yourself, bringing new ways of being, acting, and living through the power of love.

When you have given yourself the time to be in this vibration, to be-lieve this is you, you start the creative juices flowing all around you, for creation is the seed for the creativity within you. It is the passion that moves through the ever-present moment, allowing your pure essence to come to your awareness. When you have given yourself the permission to just be in your heart without judgment, you give yourself permission to be all who you are.

This will be a discovery. For the soul to discover more of itself is the mission and purpose of their life. This is the code of creation. Spirals of being and knowing are swirling and coding around you. The cycles of creation are sparked within you and connect to the universal planes of all existence. This contributes to the whole. The collective consciousness is then seeded with more light codes of you.

You are inter-connected, interwoven in all dimensions of time, space, and realities. Trust that your soul and your consciousness is part of the divine plan of creation. Your code is to be shared by you, for only you have the unique code to you that is to contribute to the whole. The variations and multidimensional aspects of all creation are sprinkled with many seeds of individuation. This allows the singularity to become part of the whole. This is dance of the cosmos and the dance on your earthly plane too, for it will continue to happen time and time again until you realize the essence of no time. In the moment of NOW, you are aligned with the master co-creator of the divine.

TRANSFORMATION—The River Flows

Imagine this geometrical diamond spinning through your DNA. This high vibrational code can be used to transform lower vibrational energy. You can use it within and without of your being, through yourself and energetic field and in any place or event. Attune to it through your intention and call on it. See it and feel it within. Open to the activation and power of the ultraviolet fire of transformation.

All can be transformed and brought back to unity consciousness through the power of love. Release your feelings of separation, dissolve your fears, and allow the flow of creation to gracefully find its way to you. Open to receive and imagine it taking place through every particle of your being on the human and quantum level, encompassing the visible and invisible, known and unknown, as you allow the transformation to occur for you.

CHAPTER 4

TRANSFORMATION THE RIVER FLOWS

WISDOM

PROFOUND KNOWING

Beloveds, your consciousness has experienced many
troubles as well as many joys. Your consciousness is ready
for more, so allow the expansion to happen. The expansion
happens in the dance, the dance of transformation. As
you set new codes and align with your core, the old can
be no more.

You are not your past. You are not your future. You are your
present creations in the NOW, so embrace this treasure. All
your experiences of pain and dismay can no longer limit you
if you choose to co-create with consciousness on this day.
Allow the new to break on free and liberate you into your
destiny, for everything you have felt and everything you
have done can be set into wisdom as you watch the rising
sun. Do not allow the old to define you, instead transform it
and fuel it into something new.

Co-create wisdom into joy on this new day. Co-create the
very code and birth a new way. Your soul is very wise as it
aligns to your higher self. Get ready as it takes speed and

travels on its way. The quantum shift is here on this day if you choose to be free and liberate thee. All you need is the willingness to feel. Feel the pain and then set it free.

The new space that you co-create will allow the new to be. Bring the infinite stream of creation into your everyday. Allow the river of light to carry thee into the vastness of the mystery. You are the alchemist who can change and be free. Allow your energy to shine as you nourish on the seas. The waters are the emotions, the movement of energy that play a song of feelings that you move through thee. Once you feel and allow it to go, you know it does not define you because you are the master of the flow. Ease and grace are your new mantra, and you move and enjoy the show.

Why do you fear what you feel? It is your energy. If you truly know the true power you have, you will realize that the energy you create can be transformed again and again. It holds those in fear of change because they feel they have no choice. But we are here to tell you the choice is yours whether to come and experience a new song.

Dive deep, Beloveds, into the unknown mystery of the heart for the answers dwell deep within if you silence the mind and sense your body and being and co-create with your light. Follow the direction that is best for you, not only from the mind, but rather a co-creation with the heart. The balance will happen, and you will align with the stars. Focus on the Master within to open to your highest potential. You are constantly changing, so bring conscious awareness through you.

You are never the way you were before. Every moment you co-create anew as you rebirth once more, time and time again, your cells rebirth according to various cycles of creation. This is the beauty of being alive, the process of experiencing, and an ever-ongoing process.

You are at the image of the universe, always experiencing the new. It sometimes may seem scary, and you may even question if this is true because all seems the same and nothing has changed. But what we are here to remind you are always recreating your way. Whether it is the same or different, you are still co-creating your life from your own lore. The power now we say is within your very hands because you are a co-creator, and you can manifest more.

And here again you may resist so often to what is being proposed. You may resist your learning and for transformation to take hold. You rather feel in control of all that you know and instead risk seeing a new day unfold.

If you choose to experience the process of transformation, you will learn to trust yourself and you will surrender control thinking you can predict all that comes to you. Instead, you will know that the power you do have is how you perceive to experience what comes your way and how to align with the highest vision for yourself and in turn share the profound knowledge that is held within all the experiences you have made throughout your journey in the cosmos.

Transformation is the basis of your learning experience. You can transform anything, as you are co-creators of your life experience. You choose whatever you want to live on how you live it.

Enjoy the ride of change, the everlasting experience of being One with all.

THE MIRRORS THAT ENLIGHTEN YOUR CONSCIOUSNESS

Everything you see and experience in your reality is the mirror of the energy you hold. It is a window into your current state of consciousness and an opportunity to grow. What is being triggered within you by the action of another or by a situation has the potential to reveal your wounds and fears. Once you can realize this, you can accept, transform, and come home. The home is the safety of love.

The key to this realization is not in the action of the other, but rather how the experience makes you feel, think, or act. You are given many opportunities to see another or a situation as the mirror. In this mirror, you will be able to project with consciousness instead of reflecting back blame, shame, or guilt. This has been an old habit of humanity, and the cycle continues until one is ready to co-create with consciousness to empower the master within.

You have been brought-up with the sense of separation, and at times you have experienced feeling alone, different, and the need to defend yourself. In turn, you have created a fear of others.

The basis of the universal law of reflection and the law of attraction is that all is connected and part of the One. All human beings are deeply connected and have experiences that are part of the whole. In the consciousness of separation, the ego will at times push the fault onto another or punish the self with guilt. The ego in its need to protect will wish to make someone responsible as in most karmic relationships where archetypal roles of victim, perpetrator, or savior are played out. In this relationship, one is dependent on the other to prove one is worthy. Love is conditional.

Once you start to open to the possibly that you are a co-creator and that you attract your daily experience, you start to slowly release the judgment you have for others and especially yourself. Remember that what you judge in another, you hold unconsciously the same judgment toward yourself and often more intensely. All this comes from your past and the way you understood things when you were a child with an undeveloped understanding. In this childlike understanding, you believed that all that happened around you was your fault even if it was not.

This has created a protective mechanism that pops up every time you feel threatened in any way. It happens automatically just as an old habit that is completely unconscious. As, so very often, not being fully present in your body and in the present moment, one does not take time to feel with what one is truly feeling. Instead, the feelings inside build up and stay as they are, whether they are pleasant or not. This is the frequency and vibration that you hold which is often heavy and dense. As you become more aware, you will lighten or en-lighten your frequency. You will feel lighter, less burdened, and more aware.

This energy that is yours will come into interaction with the others around you. Your field goes way beyond your physical body. As you enter the field of another, you enter an interaction that will mirror to you what is inside you.

As all living beings are connected, some will come into your daily life to show you the unbalanced energy you hold inside. This will take place whether you like it or not, as you are a collective that is growing into a more conscious living and everyone is helping each other to evolve, to release their burdens, heal their wounds, and open to more love and compassion as a group.

Therefore, co-creation is a gift and is crucial for the development of the group's consciousness. Your relationships with others are a gift to help you resolve what is wounded within you. The more powerful and painful emotion triggered within you, the more ancient and unconscious is your conditioning. Nothing happens without purpose. You ALREADY hold the keys to solve it, even if you probably do not think so.

Set the intention to understand what is going on inside. Connect the dots to the missing links. Love yourself just the way you are without judging yourself or another. Give thanks for the precious gift of introspection that was offered to you. Take a distance if needed from another, while you reflect and discover what is going on inside. Ask the invisible world to help you receive more clarity on this path of expansion of consciousness. Ask to receive the signs and understanding and where you can help yourself feel safe.

This process is an individual process. Take the time needed. You will learn, you will heal, and you will allow your inner wisdom to guide you. This process cannot be rushed nor controlled. It is your evolutionary process that will take you on a journey to become more loving and caring to yourself and to others.

At times it takes a push to move out of one pattern into another. The mind is comfortable with what it knows. The mind does not honor the unknowing for the ego mind is in fear and gets lost in a state of forgetting. The mind forgets the unlimited capacity that you are connected to and are made from. Instead, it sees itself as separate and needs to battle the hardships alone.

You are not alone. You are connected to the unlimited source of all creative potential. Wisdom is drawn upon the inner depths that are beyond understanding and knowledge. Wisdom is the inner knowing despite what is happening in the physical. As you sense and feel the flow of the mystery, the light codes of conscious creation are activated.

The motion of the e-motion allows you to move through the tides if you allow the mind to cease judgment and instead focus on the co-creation. Awareness is key. That is all. It is not to fix or understand the logical, sequential reason for why. Instead, it is to bow to the mystery and allow trust to fortify within you.

Here, in this state, you are more receptive and open. Your mind softens and you are willing to listen and notice the signs and messages your soul and higher self is trying to send to you, for your soul's journey is to create more of itself through the expansion of its energetic centrical force that moves through all creation.

The co-creator's journey is the movement of wisdom through the mystery and through life itself without conditions. As a co-creator, you are required to call on your strength and courage to be willing to keep your heart open to love. This ultimately allows the wings of grace to bring you into the freedom of manifesting your creations.

CRISIS, AN OPPORTUNITY TO CHANGE

Beloved Ones in times of great change and even chaos you may question and compare what was and what is. You reflect on what is working and what is not working. When things cannot be predicted despite all your attempts to control, we ask you to consider pausing and observing. Focus on awareness and release your repressed feelings to heal and transform.

If you look carefully back on your life, you will notice that when you experienced challenges you also experienced new opportunities. Of course, during a time of crisis, it is sometimes nearly impossible to rejoice as you are in pain and you are suffering. Life is challenging you and pushing you to grow, expand, and become aware.

However, we ask you to take moments of gratitude during times of challenge and know that you can take an entirely new path. Instead of filling with fear and doubt, cease the opportunity and co-create a new way of being. You are creative beings, very powerful indeed, you are the masters of evolution, and you will succeed. You might think it took you ages and you often doubted and suffered, but despite this you have the resources inside to become stronger.

In times of crisis, reflect on the beliefs and programs that you hold within that do not serve you. Where have you chosen to dismiss your guidance and your longings for something new? Consider looking closely at any imbalances you have created in your life. Where have you given too much without opening to receive? Where have you overcompensated instead of resting and rejuvenating your body, mind, and soul?

Remember, crisis is a call for change. It is time for innovation and creativity to come join in life's game. Find the balance between your mind and your heart. As you open to a more balanced way of being with yourself and others, you open to the potentiality for something more blissful and beautiful. Begin the dialogue with others as you nurture and bring loving care to yourself. Bring the gift of the ages into the reality and co-create a land that is fair.

Be here now. The busyness of life can make you ungrounded and lost.

You are in a game of polarities fighting one against the other. The game to be WON/ONE is not to be the victor over the other. Step out of the game, beloveds, and restore into the clarity of you. Come into the middle—the balance of the two.

The imbalance tips the scales time and time again, but, eventually, it will find balance in the middle again. Which side do you choose, one or the other? There are some who take a stand in the opposite of the other and yet there are those who choose to stand in the middle without pitting one over the other. For they realize that no one can win in the opposite game because even though their positions are different, the energy is the same. The fighting will continue, and things will remain the same until one steps into the middle, the zero point with no blame.

Those that are called to resonate the energy of balance are here to gain insight into the vastness of creation. They are here to work with and realize the magnitude of the power of creation. In this zero-point field, the carbon changes form into the crystalline energies of evolvement taking form.

You can feel the subtle changes within your mind, within your body, and in your core. It will change your emotional field and neutralize it once more. The transformational process will catapult you into the new. You will awaken to your artistry that is unique to only you.

Be wise and discern in a crisis point. Stay calm and breathe in a crisis point. Allow the energy of the now to be within your field of awareness. Allow the energy of One to be All there Is.

> Chime into the hum
> Chime into the Om
> Let the sound resonate
> To bring forth your node.
>
> Many, many people say
> That the Beloved is away
>
> But as you begin to play
> The conscious co-creative way
>
> You will build a newer way
> On the earth for all to say
> Hooray!

FLOW OF CREATION

FINDING THE BALANCE BY MANAGING YOUR ENERGY SYSTEM

Energies that are vibrating at the same frequency will be attracted to each other. You resonate the frequency that you hold, and this is what you create in your life. If you do not like what you see in your life, you can change it, for you are co-creator of your universe. What you focus your energy on is what is created. You can confront what comes before you with keen eyes of awareness. You can see things as haphazard and react to all that comes your way, or you can be present in awareness and shift and change your perceptions in the moment it occurs.

It has been this misconception that you have no control of your environment. It has been taught that the need to defend and survive are all that you need to do in the world, but what we are offering to you now is the empowerment to see a new way and perceive the life you wish by changing the choices that you make with the full knowledge and awareness that you can shape all that comes before you. You can then choose to see things, situations, and people in a different light.

Nothing comes from out there to harm you. Nothing is here to create pain and suffering. You experience fear when you are projecting the wounds that are within you. Instead of feeling light and empowered, you are delving in the lower dimensions trying to control and manipulate energies to have what you want, but often unsuccessfully.

Transcend by staying fully present and conscious. Open to the unlimited source of the universe and allow it to pour through you, to assist you with its benevolence. Trust in the magnification of source and embody the creation energy within you. Trust that you are this shining light and become a powerful co-creator aligned to the better good of all, with a perfect purity in your intention, accessing this limitless and eternal power of creation in you.

Your soul does not test you nor seeks to challenge you. Divine orchestration is always loving, caring, and benevolent. Your ego sometimes tests you by judging the experience that moves into your reality. Your soul has been preparing you to hold more consciousness. Your ego's fears may generate dis-ease and suffering through the unconsciousness behaviors, resistances, and limited belief systems. It is certain that would you have known the powerful creator that you are, you would not have created it in that way.

Remember that through the process of ascension, you will always be moving, becoming more of who you truly are. This will allow more ease and grace to enter your field, allowing your core energy to flood through your life, creating much more joy, beauty, abundance, and love. You will allow your inner wisdom to guide your creations.

It is also through the process of descension that your higher light can come down and merge into your physical body, changing your body from mostly carbon-based into more crystalline-based.

The creation process is quite simple. What you think, you create. Yet, the journey of this discovery is the diligence and courageous that is needed to live a more empowered life as a conscious co-creator. What you feel affects your vibration. Your frequency calls in the experience and you attached a thought or belief to the feeling. This energy creates a field around you that affects your reality, what you perceive, and how you interact with the world.

Consider focusing on your well-being, on your abundance, your love, or on any other energy that you would like to live in; that is what you really ARE. Live the dream and shift all that you have known into something greater, more sustaining, and empowering.

Beautiful Ones come and sit with us. Breathe deeply and feel the weight of your body. Sink into your body—your beautiful, beloved body. When you come into this center point, you will start to experience your energy field. You will start to create an intimate relationship with the energy of you. You may think that energy outside of you is all there is and that you can only react and deal with the energies around you. But we say to you, the ultimate liberation is the knowing and the relationship you have with the energy of you.

The true energy of you is waiting for you to know it more fully. When you begin to start a conscious relationship with your energy field, you start to understand what your energy is and what is another, what is your energy or what is the energy of a location. This truly is a time of liberation because when you know your energy and what is not, you are able to maneuver through the tides of the collective energies that pulse in and out of all creation. Here you get to choose streams of energy for your conscious co-creation.

Know your energy. Sit in the silence. Know our energy.
When you sleep, you come into your energy. Find time
in your day to sit with yourself and consciously bring your
attention to your energy.

Start with breathing from the core of your being and allow
this energy to circulate around you with every breath.
Feel the energy around you with each and every breath
that you take.

Start to build this relationship. You will come into the
knowing. You will be skilled in maneuvering through the
unknown. You will find and become the living light portal
that you are.

MOVING WITH THE FLOW

To move with the flow of life is not always an easy process,
but it is the key to allow something new to come into your
life. You will practice this over and over again until you get
find the flow.

What is the flow? The flow is the energy all around you.
When you can sense the subtleness of the life all around
you, you are able to access the pure potential of creation.
The way into the flow is through the breath and being
present in the moment. In the presence of the moment, you
connect to All That Is.

In the present moment, as you connect with your breath,
your fears and limitations do not interfere with the currents
of life you can connect, allowing the flow of creation energy
to respond to what you call for or what you intend. This is

how you start to shape and co-create your reality because you connect to the universal flow of light.

To change something in your life or to create something new, your soul will pulse you forward; it may take the shape of uneasiness because you do not know, but instead of feeling anxious, we ask you to relax and go with the flow to allow inspiration and curiosity to guide you. When you make the conscious choice to be curious and align with the energy of discovery, you are *in-spirit* or inspired because you are connected to your higher self and the universe around you.

Inspiration is the higher frequencies of light. It is the flow of the universe. Now all you need is to act without the distraction of the mind to control the flow. Instead, move with the flow by staying fully present as you connect with your higher self.

Where does this inspiration come from? It comes from your inner knowing, this very conscious and present part of you that is fully aligned to the most prosperous outcome possible. This guidance is available to all, as you are all divine in essence and in matter. Your capability of receiving information is an ongoing process.

Usually, it is fear and the state of mind you are in that triggers an opportunity to transform. If you do not bring in conscious co-creation, you are likely to repeat the same experience you do not desire. This will cease when you consciously say NO more and affirm that you have learned what you needed to learn. You consciously choose to co-create experience that is more fulfilling and empowering.

This, of course, does not happen overnight, for it is a process. Life is a process of discovery. When you are having completed the lesson, you can choose to move on. As you maneuver through the unknown, your skills and intuition will get stronger. You will draw on the very safety of your relationship with self and you feel more adept at maneuvering through the unknown, step by step, day after day.

Bring your intention in, and state out loud that you are ready for something new. Allow life to bring you the information and teachings you need to move into the dream you envision for yourself. It does not matter how big or seemingly impossible for your mind to comprehend. Feel it. Envision it and open to receive.

Allow your inner guidance to be pulsed by the heart to explore the movement of your body into the action and nonaction. Explore what it is to give and to receive in balance by noticing the flow of contraction and release. Be the living prayer as you dream your life into being. You will be pulsed forward. You will be guided to release all the unconscious patterns that you no longer want to experience, and you will co-create something new.

This will lead you to parts of your beingness that you did not even know were there. You will discover parts of you that have been injured, broken, and even torn apart that are ready to be acknowledged and restored. This will place you on the journey of self-discovery that will bring you back to your truth. It will allow you to stand in your authenticity without hiding behind a mask where you once tried to be something that you are not and have never really been.

It is through the surrendering and the loving of self that you will heal all the wounded parts of self that are calling to be heard and that need your loving support to be loved just the way they are—LOVED BY YOU!

Activate your DREAM. Pray to be taken on the PATH OF CHANGE.

PRESSURE OF TIME

Have you noticed that sometimes you have the impression of lacking time to do all that you want to do? We wish to remind you that you do not have to entangle with this experience of lack of time, as time only exists in the third dimension. It is when you feel stressed and are overwhelmed with your emotions that you lack time. When you sit in this level of consciousness, there is a need to control, and all seems to slip from your hands.

Choose to take yourself out of the perception that you lack time. Lack automatically implies the fact that you are waiting for the experience to happen, so in fact you are calling the exact experience that you wish to avoid. Instead, consider choosing to take a step back to discover a way that releases this pressure. Ask for support, Beloveds. Call in the benevolent universe that supports you and sends signs to open to a new way of perceiving. Stop and breathe. Bring in the presence of the now moment. This will allow all the rushing of the mind to cease.

The moment you allow space around yourself to take a breath and say, "I don't need to decide or do this in this instant," you allow an opening to receive more clarity through consciousness and awareness. In that state of being, you will know when you need to know or do.

By allowing space within, you refuse to stress yourself and decide that this is an opportunity to learn how to honor yourself and manage your emotions. Instead of rushing, you allow the divine flow to take care of everything. Ask for support, call in your angels and/or guides who will help you organize your thoughts and bring clarity once again. Practice self-care by doing things that will release the pressure and open to higher states of consciousness where there is clarity, certainty, and confidence. Soon, you will discover that new ideas or the answer you were looking for just comes to you, allowing all to unfold beautifully with divine grace and total trust.

To navigate in a higher level of consciousness, choose to step out of the arena of stress and chaos and come into the presence of the now.

Beloveds, time is an illusion. We say this because you can shift into the different timelines of creation. In the ever now moment, you can access the timelessness of no time. Herein lies your liberation. Once you can focus and bring your attention to your breath and allow the pause to be in the certainty of the test, you will understand that more can happen in an instant and more can be achieved in a moment of no time or in the presence of the now.

When you bring your attention to the ever now moment instead of what you lack, the expansion of time works with you instead of against you. All is in the flow of everlasting love, and you will awaken more of yourself as you bring in love to thee.

Love is never ceasing, always gentle, and has no end. When you allow this state of being to flow through you, you access the stream of energy that flows with all time, all dimensions as well as the space around you.

Allow this magical place to be part of your reality. You are the co-creator of this existence and so, too, can you maximize the time you are in by being fully in the moment of now.

EMBRACE CHANGE

IN A TIME OF BIG CHANGE

A major shift in consciousness occurs as the currents of your time begin to destabilize your earthly structures and you are called back to the core essence of being human. You are now experiencing the climax of the imbalance and are forced by worldwide events to look deeply within.

The world as you knew it no longer is, and a new beginning is here. What will you do now to shape a living seed into the glory of a day you are to behold? Come now and wonder with us. Tell a new story for all to be told, for as many awaken to their souls call the manifestation of love can open many doors.

Breathe now and let the thoughts fall away. You cannot predict when all is in dismay. Find your center within your heart and allow the brevity of time to expand into a spark. The spark of light will ignite as you breathe and focus on the center of love to be the deed. What is it that you love?

What is awakening within you? Find the solace not in the chaos but in the peace within you.

As you shift your awareness from the mind to the heart, allow the lullaby to calm you as you untie the knots.

Your frequency will increase. Your vibration will be high. The natural forces within the evolutionary cycle increase the vibration high. Mother Earth resonates at a higher vibe too. You are One with the planet because the planet is within you. You are made up of the elements and as change does come to you, remember you are equipped to alchemize the dark into the light just as the sun rises too.

Time seems to fly by. The acceleration is here. You are doing much more within minutes and in hours. More in little time seems now the norm. Time has been stretched like a rubber band, but it will come in as the rotations change hands. The increase of the vibration affects everything too. It changes your body, your beliefs, and your memories too. It may bring up past traumas that arise from deep within you.

You are experiencing an upgrade to your energy system. Plasmic light is flooding the world through. Your body and the earth are integrating these energies too. You cannot cancel or put it on stop. The planets and the stars are part of you too. Become conscious and heal if you choose. The change is coming whether you see it or believe it or not.

Release now your ego's fears and drop the need to prove you were something more. You have competed and have fought to show all your worth and now the wars within you are created around you. You do not need to tell others that you are worthy, so only your belief in yourself will be the show. Do you like what you see? If you do not, change it within thee. The inner reflects the outer, and on and on we go. If enough of you believe in your holy place, the magic will surely show.

Change brings up the very fears for many, we say, but realize that too your brother and sister feel the same way. You may run, shout, and fall to your knees, but we say all will change when you help those in need.

Humanity has initiated wars and ensued chaotic nodes. You have been accustomed to focusing on the satisfaction of your needs, wants, and desires instead of peace within your true home.

You have looked outside of yourself to fulfill the void. It has made you believe that something or someone outside of the self can stop this hunger. Many have rushed and scrambled to find it in the busyness of the day only to be disappointed because love cannot be sustained by drawing upon a limited supply of someone else's dismay. It is only within one's own heart that one can draw from true divine co-creative potential, the unlimited source of love.

As the frequency increases and the atomic particles move faster, you are challenged to step out of the position of who is right and who is wrong. You are being asked to release the "old" way of perceiving and instead enter conscious co-creative healings.

This journey starts with you. Connect with the invisible realm of the quantum field all around you. Enter the truth of the light and love that you are.

This process of change is happening, whether you want it or not. It is taking place. We remind you again that you cannot control nor stop it. We are here to guide you to release your resistances. We are here to help you know true surrender and forgiveness, for surrender is not a giving up, but rather a conscious co-creative stance to build up with force. The force is connected to unlimited source creation. May the force be with you, within you and aligned to your very core in conscious co-creation to live your gift and adore the many aspects of variety that ones can use to play. Open to the potential without shunning it away. It is your choice. You get to choose, but remember that others get to choose too.

If you resist, the fear may arise. It may be feelings of loss and spiraling out of control. You may be in the dark and do not know which way to go, but light within your heart will show you where you need to go. Your body may hurt, and your mind may be filled with intense hate. You may act in negatives patterns and feel disgrace. A victim, you stand as others take you for granted; they are concerned too and only want to get on top of the ladder.

If you choose to surrender to the unknown, day after day, you will learn to move within your bones. You will be your most authentic self. You will step out of the old and liberate yourself.

During periods of major change, choose to respond instead of reacting with a hot head. Consciously co-create and be free of old patterns of conditioning and unrest. The ego's need to protect you is then relieved. It can take a step back and finally breathe. You will then align your ego and your soul. You will marry the beauty that you hold. Remember one is not better than the other, but the balance between the two. Come into the center, the zero point of the true you.

The energetic space within you is freed to explore to be the master co-creator and much more. You will be able to transform the old dense energy within thee into something consciously creative that is inspired within thee. It will be fueled with the firelight of love. It is efficient and effective, built with laser-light focus, because you listened to the wisdom of the soul. The power of source creation is your nourishment at hand. You have chosen to open to a new life and to co-create a new land.

To keep your vibration light and resonant with your soul, activate gratitude and bow with what you know. You can raise your vibration high by opening your heart. Your gifts will be revealed in the starry bright light. You are a living light portal pouring grace through and through. You know your supply comes from the unlimited Source of pure potential. You are able share freely without hesitation, for the life force expands in the exponential.

Sit centered in yourself and focus on your heart. Activate the power of gratitude. Think of all the things you are grateful for. Let it come in like a magnet drawing all goodness to you. Place your attention and awareness on the vibration of your heart. Activate the coherence of your center. Gift yourself with the love you need to feel safe, present, and loved. Thank life for all it has already provided you and concentrate on increasing the vibration within you. Broadcast this resonance out to humanity and sit in this new consciousness of love. It is reflected in all that you create and co-create.

Choose to transform what you see and feel by opening your heart to heal. Decide the goal you wish to achieve and in what direction you wish to go. Remember that you co-create your life and that nothing happens without purpose. Sometimes, you encounter difficult and painful experiences, but if you become conscious and use it as a teaching, it can be fuel to ultimately serve the highest good for your evolution of consciousness. Become the observer and profoundly change your life in magical ways. When you do, you change the world.

It is time to take flight and enter the new age of light. Are you willing to go in between the spaces of time and travel through the darkest parts of your mind? If so, you may discover that you will come out in the end into the lightness of your heart, for no matter how you travel, you will always come back to your core, as your very essence is able to expand and grow more. The single most challenge that one faces during times of change is the resistance to life and the ebbs and flows of the waves. But make no mistake the magic we say is in the conscious co-creation because it is naturally flexible and magnetically powerful in the game.

As the movements of your creations begin to take shape, discover and reflect if this is where you are to rate. For you will always get to revise it, redefine it, and move it along. Choose to shift it on the many threads of light, for your creation is your energetic code of light. Do not judge, rather witness the movement into form. Be the artist, the scientist of your creations into form.

If you wish to experience something else, well then move and shift the pattern along. Move it along and transform into creation light of love's pure delight. Allow your willingness to see the balance of light and dark that is within thee.

Allow the pain to be and the comfort of love to ease all these emotions and anxieties of thee, for nothing is forever and forever is all. In the movement of all things, there is always something more. It is never the same, always something more. Time and time again, something can be born. Change the pattern and restore the diamond light to the core.

There is always something to be gained when one reflects with care. There is always something to learn when one slows down and wants to share. For you came here to be the starlight of love and you will forever cast a shadow on that too afar. One will be with the other if one chooses to co-create into form. The polarities will come together and bring forth the form.

As one holds, the other gives; as one sings, the other sits, for you are all here to witness the strings of light that you hold. You play the game together and pick each other up when you fall. Why do you shame and blame others? Why don't you all come together into the heart for all?

You go. You come. You trail away on and on. But we say force not. Come into the stone's toss and see the ripples that you create along the way.

How do you fly when you do not know you have wings? We say stop and get out of the mind, but rather into the body and open your wings!

Beloveds, what has always been waiting is for you to feel free, is the heart to know love as one sings their story to thee.

Love without condition, judgment, or shame is now the story in this new plane. Open yourself up and receive this bountiful grace. Your wings are now opening. Your heart calls to discover. Fly now, be free, and explore. Empower your light into your very core.

Come now and witness the starry light day
The child wants to witness
the beauty of this new way
Come now and listen

to the silence of the heart
Beyond the whispers
the sparkle
sings the brilliance of a light heart
Open
Soften
See
Open
Soften
Be
Beauty and grace now are
All you will ever need

WHAT TO DO IN TIMES OF GREAT CHALLENGES?

What are you to do when you experience great challenges? We say to you, release the fear and pray!

You are not powerless. Realize that it is only the past and the uncertainty of the future that creates stress and fear in your existence. Your power resides in your willingness to release your past traumatic experiences. Notice your additions to drama and instead be the living prayer of conscious co-creation.

As the living prayer, you open your heart and you raise your frequency and vibration. It opens you to the quantum field of all possibility. You start focusing on what you really want because you can step out of the fear or the lack of what you do not want.

Your prayer will activate the space around you. It will free your mind from having to solve everything. It will cease to fret to seek a solution. Your heart frequency will increase and the higher vibrations of the wisdom of the heart will carry you. Through the asking for assistance, you will receive the help from the invisible world. Synchronicities will occur which will allow you to see the blessings that are ready to come your way. You are free from the fear of uncertainty.

Beloveds, be the living prayer. The prayer is the conscious awareness of where you put your thoughts and intentions. The power of prayer is the power of your intention you put into it. The energetic force of creation can move through all that is as well as within you. This is the power that it holds.

Prayer can change your frequency and vibration and allow you to come into the peace of love. Your body is the instrument for the breath to move. When you bring awareness to the breath and the body, the prayer takes shape at a powerful level. It allows your body to remember its purity. It allows your body to align with the many parts of you that are not seen that is part of your consciousness.

In times of great challenges, you become confused and reactive. So, we ask you to do the opposite of rushing about and to consciously slow down. Instead, focus on your breath and then focus on your heart center. You will start to ground within your body and move out of fear. Here lies the access point of your higher self and your higher knowing.

In this place, you cease control. You surrender to your divinity, for in your higher knowing is the wisdom to confront all that is before you as you transform your fears into the breath. The transformation happens when you cease control, surrender, and allow the flow. You allow your feelings to come to the surface and you ask a higher power to take the burdens from you and ask for help.

You are in this state of awareness knowing that you are not alone, for when you pray, you connect to the higher vibrations of creation energy. This energy that moves through you enables you to see other possibilities and solutions without trying so hard to do so, for the power of prayer does not cease when you stop prayer. The energy of the prayer is with you. You begin to fortify your field and allow your higher self to connect with your ego. You co-create with your ego and instead of reacting from fear you can hear the higher guidance of your Soul.

Prayer and meditation can be the same. Do not get caught up in the vernacular. Instead, understand that your prayer is unique to you. Your prayer may be a walk in the park or a time of focusing on your senses and not on your thoughts. You may call it a pause. You may call it downtime. It does not matter what you call it. Just allow the racing mind and your thoughts to fall away. Breathe in the very breath of life that is here to sustain you. That is all. All is that—round and round we go. Where we stop, nobody knows, but around and around we go. Breathe and surrender to the higher knowing of you.

CAN THE MIND AND THE FEELINGS BE CONTROLLED?

Liberate your mind and your feelings by releasing the need to control them. So often, we hear you say that you would like another to love you and you have tried to make this happen. You have experienced that whatever you do or not do, how much you try to please it is never under your control. It never has been and will never be, for you have no control over what another feels or thinks. You can only take care of yourself and how you feel and what you think about yourself.

Regarding your own mind and feelings, here again you cannot control what you think and feel. The only thing you can do is that through your awareness. Be present in the given moment and train your mind to manage your emotions by responding with the care of self.

If you choose this path, you will dedicate some time on a regular basis by slowing down and going within. You will consciously connect with your breath and may practice any other meditative tool, as it will not happen on its own. This practice will bring you more stability, more clarity and provide the necessary distance between what is happening to you and how you choose to respond. You will be able to monitor your thoughts and emotions.

We encourage you to check regularly in your day to see where your thoughts are. How are you feeling? This will enable you to be more present in the moment, so that you can be more connected with what you see, smell, touch, and taste. Take the time to live more consciously.

Beloveds, you have tried to master the control of the mind and the emotions. You have tried to suppress what comes through you. The suppression is the blocks. As you cease control, you allow your thoughts and feelings to move through you instead of staying stuck within you.

The control that you put yourself under is the illusion that you are safe. In your uncertainty and doubt, your heart closes to love. If you can understand that to control is to hold the very thing you are running from, you will start to be aware that you truly have no control. You will realize that surrendering this control is liberating, for you are safe and you do not need to know everything. Rather, you are more curious and open to discovery just as a child is open to the new moment to moment.

You run your thoughts through your mind. You try to figure out what is between the lines; around and around the cycle goes. Where it stops, nobody knows. Your mind is confused and wants to BLOW! So, cease control and let it go. Allow the memories to go. You are not your past and you are not the future. Be here now. The now is you.

PURE LIGHT

OVERCOMING FEAR

When fear arises, do not let it overwhelm you, as if you do so, your experience becomes more painful.

We suggest that the first thing you ask yourself is, "Am I in immediate danger?"

Through the expressing of this question, you take a distance from the fear and come back to the reality of the present moment. As when the answer to this question is, most times, "No," you realize that that this is a construct of your mind.

If you are not in imminent danger, fear is usually based on past experiences that have left an imprint in your physical body where a feeling of hopelessness may arise when you felt vulnerable, hurt, or wounded. This past experience whether it be in this life or on the long experience of existence throughout your soul's journey, is present in your physical body and is calling for help.

As the physical body is the body through which you experience all of life, it stores all the memories regardless of the timeline. It does not distinguish when this experience took place; it stores the emotion, the pure vibration, and the intensity what is lived. You can distinguish two types of E-motion, energy in motion.

The first type of e-motion is beneficial for the body. It brings in peace, serenity, and love. It is stored in your body as resolved energy, which maintains its purest vibrational state of love and helps the body relax.

The second type of e-motion is a vibration that stresses the body. The mind activates the brain to find a way out of an immediate danger. It activates the mind, as the body cannot distinguish if this fear is real in the now or comes from the past. In this moment, take the action to ask, "Am I in immediate danger? Is this here now?"

As you step out of the illusion of the danger, you can start breathing and relaxing more and more through the power of the breath of life. You can take the necessary steps to restore the balance in your body and allow your fear to be released. It is a bit like taking care of a little child who sees the world around him or her so big and feels powerless, even though it is not the reality of the energy that surrounds the experience.

Through the breath, call in your sacred masculine, this powerful God presence, this energy of protection. Call in your masculine energy to stay focused on the truth of the moment and on what energy you really wish to live in the moment. Release old unresolved e-motions that arise from the past. These energies only wish to be released out of your physical body to restore the peace through the new consciousness of love and forgiveness.

Sit, if you need, in the releasing of the old, assisted and protected by your sacred masculine self that is here for you. It will bring you the strength to stay focused on the dream you wish to anchor and release any unresolved experience that is stored in your physical body from times where you did not stay focused on your dream and was therefore unable to anchor your dream in your life and unable to live your gifts.

YOU ARE READY FOR THESE TIMES OF CHANGE

You have trained throughout all time and evolution. You have prepared to be the pioneers of change. This is a fascinating phase of the development of the world and humanity. It is an opportunity to create a whole new reality.

Co-creator you are the thoughts and feelings you vibrate. In every moment, you are radiating a combination of energetics to the field around you as the quantum field responds to you by amplifying your creation. You are ready for quantum creations.

Your conditioning over many generations has been the consecration of the mind. However, now it is time to discover that it is the heart that guides the mind and not the other way around.

When you choose to be present and connect your heart to your profound gratitude, you open to the power of love that sits within you. Your heart is a multidimensional portal that expands your experience. You expand in all directions as you connect fully with the quantum field. As you share your vibration with your mind, your perception changes as you free yourself from the activity of the mind.

Beloveds, the time of big change creates a crisis point in your reality. In this reality of crisis, all comes out of the pattern you have created for yourself. You are now forced to bring your awareness on adapting to a new energetic and thus the predictability is lessened, and you are traveling in the unknown.

Whether you are traveling in your states of consciousness or in the physical realm in which you live, no matter, because the micro is the macro, and all can be gained from the knowledge that you are part of the whole eternal creation game. Understand that you are surely equipped to understand that many dynamics that you built upon in this game. Time and time again, you received the inklings to create a new code into existence. Your soul will surely be pulsed to co-create again and again.

How fast or how slow is up to you. Nobody knows—the lover is you. How will you live and what will you co-create? Everything you ever need is full of bounty if you understand your fate.

Your fate is to live, love, and co-create. Recreate again and again. It is never ending; never ceasing it is the eternal game.

FEAR OF FEAR OR NEGATIVITY

You are conditioned to be afraid. So many fears are not real they were given to you during your childhood through your family lineage and the society in which you were born. Through these fears you developed the habit of the need to be protected in any way possible. The biggest limitation is the fear of the fear.

Fear can only be released if you accept to face it. It is only when fear arises and that you ask yourself, is it true? Am I really in danger? If not, then where does it come from?

It is then with true awareness that you can choose if you need it or not anymore. Are you willing to dissolve it? Often you will discover that it is your mind that is in need to control. By allowing the mind to relax, by choosing to not allow the fear to be an obstacle, you can allow yourself to move through it and beyond.

When you raise your consciousness, you move deeply within into a completely new experience far beyond the physical place where your mind can go. You rise into a space of unity and completeness. In these higher dimensions, duality does not exist, so, in higher dimensional consciousness, nothing can be misused, and nothing can harm you. Therefore, it is free of any separation, fear, negativity, and need of protection.

By stepping into a higher level of vibration, through the powerful energies of love that are your innate intelligence, you will discover that your original and purest energy reside in the center of your heart. You will be equipped to co-create in a dimension that holds lower frequencies and, despite this, marry the two into One.

Beloveds, we know that the mind has taken precedence over your reality for so long. You have forgotten your pure divine nature by accessing the heart. So, we say to you, yes, you will feel fear, but despite this, do it anyway.

Sometimes, the breath will help you move through the fear, sometimes walking right through the fire of fear is an action that must be taken. You will feel, think that is much more to it, but, despite what you think, we say to you, you can overcome the fear by accepting that fear will arise and fall as you continue this plane of existence.

As you bring more and more awareness to yourself and
you start to understand the patterns you have created,
you will understand that you are able to recreate, and your
empowerment of love will surely win over the fear.

Be gentle. Know that fear will be there, but understand
it is what you choose in those moments of fear that will
transform it all back into the light of love, if so, you dare.

EXPANSION—Wisdom of the Ancients

You are a spiritual being that has the gift of experiencing life in many forms. Your soul holds a unique journey and has learned and experienced many things. You have traveled throughout the cosmos and hold precious gifts for you and humanity. This code will allow you, as you meditate with it, to remember the reason why you are here on the earth, the mission of your soul, and what is dear to your heart.

The purpose of this code is to help you retrieve the wisdom of love that lies within you, so that you may be the truest expression of the essence of creation. You are unique; you come to share your gifts with those around you and with Mother Earth. You are here in the physical body in this given moment as you hold a key of evolution that is needed for the Golden Age to seed and birth through your consciousness, anchoring it for those around you. The wisdom you seek is within your heart center. As a cosmic being connecting with all those around you, you open to the One and only path—the path of Love.

CHAPTER 5

EXPANSION WISDOM OF THE ANCIENTS

Beloveds, how ancient it has been to discover the old ways. Now, with this wisdom, you will rediscover the greater parts of yourself by reaching to the stars. The stars hold the intelligence of the ever-present light that is seeded within your hearts as well as in Gaia.

For the essence of life eternal is expanded beyond time captured by stardust and will continue to be the particles of matter that help shape and mold the realities that you create. So, in essence, the stardust is woven within the threads of the universe to create a sound code of life that will eternally spiral into the Sun of One. For many galaxies have been created through the turning of the spiral as all life is created with the heart of One.

Breathe deeply now, knowing that you are part of the cosmos. You are part of the earth as well, for everything is One. There are many beings of light that have held other consciousness beyond your earthly plane and now you will each tap into something new to restore the brilliance of the star that spins around and around the axis point of no time.

For many can access this point if one allows the lower mind to sit calmly with stillness and allow the body to fill with

the spirals breath that moves around and around your field
as well as within the very veins you hold to help circulate
the new codes of creative potential. For your cells can be
renewed with the intention of life everlasting and so your
consciousness too is life everlasting.

We come to you in this moment and speak of ways in
which you are to come into the *beingness* of this new world
creation that has been written in the stars many eons ago.
To come into the glory means to remember the heritage
of the star stellar code that sits in the well of knowledge
that we as a collective hold. For we have brought forth this
wisdom to bring in the dawn of a new awakening. It is vast
and comes from a higher dimensional consciousness that
is beyond what you can comprehend in the lower mind.
Until the days of thunder are over and the pounding of each
other's thoughts are finally put to rest, then you take to a
new glory and work toward birthing a new world.

For the bridge is being created within your own
consciousness as you each seed a fabric of love into the
threads of light and will eventually create the tapestry that
will co-create a new blueprint of a paradigm where creative
endeavors are not limited to the mind but are activated
through the heart's call to Oneness.

For the inter-connectedness of all things will become
apparent during the waking hours of the light. You
see what you can destroy and what you can create in
collaborative light.

Those who are called to go with you will be called to be the
light bearers and love bearers of this new dawning that is
taking place within your consciousness and soon into your

physical reality as you each ground within the new codes of creation into your consciousness as well as into your physical body. New changes are occurring for you. So be gentle on yourselves and your loved ones as well as to all the beings you encounter now.

We come with great excitement and will continue to guide you to find your heart's glory of grace and purity within the twin.

The seeds you plant now are for the children even when you turn to dirt, the fertile ground will be what they walk upon. Light walk along your path, light bearers. Walk on.

EXPANSION

LEAP INTO THE UNKNOWN

To go within is to travel in the unseen world of forgetfulness. You have forgotten the truth of who you are, and the journey back is unknown territory for your ego. The soul knows the way home. We are reminding you and supporting you to honor the truth of your soul. The listening to your soul will help you maneuver back home.

Embedded deep within you are the keys to your liberation. What you seek cannot be found outside of yourself. It is only within that your truth can be sung. Find your voice of your heart's true call. You will be able to speak from the wisdom of your soul.

It may not be comfortable for you do not know which way to go. Be courageous and follow your soul. You have relied on your five senses and the venture is unknown, but now we say it is time to use the new tools you have learned on your journey to awareness. Discern, pause, and empower your intention.

The potentiality for new innovations can be found in these unknown crevices just waiting to be found. The sensation and the exhilaration of leaping into the unknown can certainly be imagined and played like the Game of Thrones. You each are the royalty of your soul. To sit upon your throne is to be sovereign in your individuation. In pure confidence, shine brilliant like a star.

Be willing to travel into this uncharted place. Each and every person will follow his or her own path. The journey is to be done by you and you alone. You may have others to show you support, but still, you are the only one who can travel his or her own path.

Maneuver into the mystery by staying open to the signs. If you must, set the intention and a symbolic gesture. Some may call a ritual and others a ceremony. It does not matter what name you give it. All we offer you is to remember to bring in the sacred.

What is sacred to you? What do you hold dear? Find the answers by discovering what priorities you are willing to put your energy toward. As you go about your day to day, ask yourself if you are in alignment with your integrity and are you okay. Find your center, dear Ones. Know thyself. This is the most important relationship you will ever have.

It will take faith. You will need to be in trust with your ability to follow your heart. Always remember that no matter what choice you make, you can always choose again. You will always be in revision as you refine your tools along the way. Closer and closer you will come into the center of knowing thee.

Along the way you will trust in the nuisances. What feels right? What feels wrong? How do I feel? Do I feel strong? All these questions bring you into the place of a path of least resistance and find ease in its place. Find the ease in the gift of the unknown by listening closely to the whispers of the soul.

The mystery entails a curious mind. It is ready to discover as the heart leads the way. An expansion of light is guaranteed. With only your willingness you shall succeed.

You can have those who inspire you to take the journey and be bold, but you are the only who can take the leap into the unknown. Using this energy in consciousness connects you to the grid of light that travels beyond this third dimensional space. In these realms of higher light follow the trail into the One heart.

Miracles will be experienced as you open to this, it is true. Believe in the miracles and it will manifest through you. Shift your perception and see a new way and behold the miracle time and time again. All you really need do is to take the risk. Do something different that your heart yearns for instead of all the stale ways to be comfortable and safe. Complacency never did anyone good, for the growth is not stirred and the passion does not flow. Your soul wants an adventure into the realms of love instead. Open now and receive this blessed grace.

The seeing is not of the physical eyes, but rather a seeing of the inner eye. It is the vision that the higher self holds for Ones great life. Once you can see beyond the veil of forgetfulness, you will be able to manage each moment in the mystery of presence.

The gateway into the heart will allow the mystery to unfold. So, as you calm your mind and breath into the body, you will travel with an up-tempo. The rhythm of your breath will be the focus atlas. Your thoughts will fall away, and peace will manifest.

The leap into the unknown is the freedom you crave. Stretch out your arms and open your heart and breath into this newfound place. The support that is needed will come from the many streams of light. You will connect the dots of this starry light.

Let the dance begin. Let the journey unfold. In this place, there is nothing to do, nothing to know, nothing to want, because all is in perfection. All will unfold through the laws of the universe as revealing the unthinkable, the unseen, and the invisible become visible.

It only takes your willingness to surrender. Release any form of control. Anchor your faith and know that nothing is against you. Nothing is here to harm you for on the contrary, in this space of the unknown, pure source creation can be found. From this all you dream of can be created. All your wishes may emerge. Compassion and love will guide your way and enable paradise on earth for all sentient beings.

Attune your body, mind, and spirit to the rhythm of the earth. Connect to the higher vibrations of consciousness. Have faith that all is possible from this space of the unknown. It is unknown by your human self, but very well-known from your soul as this is not the first time you open to the pure source of creation. Have no other agenda then moving with the flow of the universe and dance in the rhyme of life that is unfolding through the unknown.

YOU ARE NOT YOUR BODY, NOR ARE YOU THE MIND

You are not your body, nor are you the mind. Dear Ones, you are so much more!

We wish to tell you that you may take this as a mantra, repeating it over and over again, each time you feel attached or stuck, unable to lift your vibration.

Your suffering comes through your attachment to the form of your body and your beliefs. This keeps you in lower densities and vibrations. You feel heavy, burdened, and weighed down.

Detach to what you think you are and free yourself. See from a higher point of view. You repeat what you know, think, and feel that comes from the highest vision for yourself. Do not trap yourself in your limited vision of self. We wish to convey to you that there is always a choice to go down another path, a path of expansion, where you can start seeing things through a wider point of view.

It is not easy to increase your vibration when all around you is depressed, when all around you is only fear and suffering. However, it is only through your conscious choice to free yourself from this condition that you can start to elevate yourself and take the necessary distance to open to the unknown parts of yourself that bring you bliss.

Use this mantra, "I am not the body, nor am I the mind," and enjoy the freedom that it will start bringing to you. Fortify your energetic field with the frequency and vibrations of the sound of these words. As the mind ponders and considers that you are not the body or the mind, you allow space for the heart to feel and sense the truth that lies deep within.

Beloveds, you ponder who you are, what you should do, and what is your life's purpose. You try to understand what you are, but we are here to tell you that you cannot define a star. For the star has many elements and codes within and anything can be created for the seeds are nurtured within.

To define and explain over and over again, will bring you around the spiral again. For what is One's journey but to discovery and grow? It is the journey, not the destination. Don't you know? It was always to be and always will be that the soul's discovery is the pulsing to know.

Do not fret, if you do not know, just celebrate instead and the master within you will grow. When the cycles do change and you understand your light, you will get to play in pure delight. Instead of seeking approval and validation from whom you think is good, all will be revealed to you, as it should.

If you are not your body, nor a matter of your mind, what say you instead? Master un-wind! Take all your troubles and blockages to the sun and open the firelight and run,

Beloved, run. Run into the sun. For the joy will bring you more curiosity we say, and as the soul discovers, it is surely on its way. You are on the way to the light. You are on your way to love. The master co-creator is shown from the stars above and so below. You are balanced within and you are ready for the grand show.

YOU ARE NOT ALONE

Through your limited vision, you live a life of separation. You may feel separate from all others and you may feel unloved. You may even have the impression that nobody understands you and you feel disconnected from others and the universe.

This path of solitude is a very common experience. So many people live this and suffer tremendously. When you no longer can take the suffering, you start to seek solutions and are more willing to change. Inevitably, this leads you to step into the unknown. The human race, in its biology, is very frightened of the unknown. In your DNA is the memory of survival where you often were in risk of danger and of dying. In today's time, you have thrown away the physical survival kit and replaced it with the ego's survival kit born from an anxious mind. Still, the need to feel safe is real and you will do what it takes to protect yourself. Still, the journey to wholeness will continue as you travel from separation to oneness for this part of the evolutionary process.

When you no longer wish to be suffering, arise into courageousness to find a solution. Walk on this path of evolution with us and discover your direct connection to your higher self and to all the others. By accessing to this truth, you connect to our consciousness, to the spirit of your ancestors and the greater consciousness that can guide you out of separation into wholeness.

Over the last decades, many have connected to the unity consciousness that rules creation. All these beings have created a personal path and have anchored all their healing processes in the collective consciousness of humanity.

Choose to ask for the assistance of all those who have already achieved the way back home to unity within. You can accelerate your growth by riding on the river of grace and tap into all that has been healed, liberated, and transformed. Allow yourself to receive from all those before you who have transcended their limitations, all this is waiting for you to call upon it. Flow into this experience by releasing the need to know. Be ease. Be peace. You will come in and out of peace. Still, use this as leverage to accelerate your awakening of consciousness. Your body will attune each time you remember to go with the flow. And when the fear comes again, and you feel that time is ticking, you wonder what your life is if all there is, is to die. What legacies have you left? How will others get by? Have you filled up your nest?

Beloveds, you fear that all is lost when you lie to rest and die. You fear that there is nothing else and worry fills your mind. Instead of connecting and opening your heart to love, you build walls and peak through the door. You stand ready to fight the given war. You declare you will never be hurt again. You secretly will not forget even though you say you forgive, and you will try once more. You are told that forgiveness is the right thing to do, but no one has showed you how to do this forgiveness thing too.

Your relationships are based on conditions and forgiveness does not match that way because to truly to forgive is to give love despite any dismay. The only way you can travel along this path is to forgive yourself fully for creating the reality in which you live. Start by bringing love to yourself into your very core. Open your heart and courageously bring in the love through the holy door. Do this despite the condition in which you find yourself. Choose again to make revisions and consciously co-create your life from here on in.

Forgiveness is about detachment ,and you are told that is the right thing to do, and still you do not know how to forgive truly through and through. What is missing is the ability to co-create it through the mastery of you. So, you say okay, I forgive and go on with your day, but you really have not let it go because it still hurts to give it away.

You hold this burden close, and your walls are made of steel. You fear of opening your heart for the pain is very real. You live a life playing defense standing ready to uphold your ego's plan. You are ready to fight the battle with your sword ready in your hand. You at times are tired of fighting the wars within and without. You wonder if this drama will every fully play out.

Your creative potential lies dormant within the deep dark well. Each time you hurt, you stuff it back inside instead of allowing it to move through. The cycle continues because you have not received the teachings that it is to serve, your soul is screaming for you to listen, but the call remains unheard.

The teaching is to open your heart and bring love onto you. Forgiveness is to give love first before you deem it as deserving too. Judgment holds all the pain in an anxious mind. If you want to be free of this burden, relax and breathe in and sigh. All your judgments turn back at you, for others mirror the thoughts that you hold. Realize that you were blaming them for the things you could not control.

You use your energy to protect yourself and to try to make others understand. You realize that it is not for them but for you to fully comprehend that you are trying to convince yourself that you are worthy of love's grand plan. Beloveds, you do not know what we know. You are a blazing angel star. We are made from creative light and hold the magic in your hands. You are worthy of loves divine plan in the oneness of all there is, and you are here to manifest your individual gifts to bring harmony and peace upon the land.

As you ponder and start to connect to the blessing of the real you, your soul will stir with the inklings of will be ready to co-create with you. You cannot sleep so you go outside and see all the stars in the night sky. You make a wish and intend to see all the signs and synchronicities. You hear the whispers of your soul to connect and find your light. You find the courage to know what it is to fly in the starry night.

As you develop this relationship within your holy star self, you will awaken to realize the truth that what you seek in another is really within you. Dive deep within the silence of the presence of the moment. Call to the many parts of you that you have lost because of shame. Bring them back with gentleness and forgive yourself for shunning them away. Embrace them into your very heart to be whole once again and allow these parts to join with you and discover a new way.

You are the only one who can co-create with the higher you. The single most important thing is to nurture the relationship within you. To nourish another, you must learn how to nourish you.

It was never about anyone else; it is always about you. This is not in selfishness, rather, a self-full deed to choose. It is only in arrogance when the ego needs to prove it is true. The soul needs no convincing to the divine truth of you. Self-fullness requires humility that is willing to honor another's plan. It is in the honoring of all, that together we can co-create a plan.

Separation is an illusion in your inner eye—the eye that can see beyond the third dimensional cries. This battle within the self has created wars, struggles, and strife. It is time to raise your vibration into a higher octave of light. You are not alone. We are here with you. When all seems blue, we encourage you to remember the love of a friend, the smile of a child, and your lover with whom you share your bed. For these things are not silly at all, when you understand that all are One. Together, we weave a greater consciousness around the earth to ascend. Gaia will join her family in the cosmos beyond this land.

INNOVATION

EMBRACING ALL—THE SEED OF KNOWING

All your answers are within the heart portal of One. For creation has come from the seed of knowing and now the birthing is becoming. You are feeling the contractions of this new birth. You are in labor and you doubt whether you can endure to see it manifest on the earth.

But we say to you, this creation will be birthed. It does not come from the ego mind. Be in the moment you will know what to do, just feel, sense, breathe, and move into another spiral of you. Pause when you need to and follow again with steady speed. Push, release, and move forward as the tides move out to the sea.

You cannot control the rhythm for all is part of life. The change is occurring. It cannot now stop. The momentum is building whether you try to control it or not. All is part of the game for the liberation of life to appear, for we are the only ones that can make sense of it by transforming our fears.

The wheel of fate is turning as the cycles do run its course. Around and around, you circle the sun, another rotation is in full force. Your expectations are your struggles. Drop them, we say. Be in love with the moments of spontaneity and exhilaration. Allow life to be the treasure as you bring in gratitude instead.

Connect with us now. Dear Hearts, breathe. Feel the grace pouring in as you stabilize with ease. Connect now to Gaia. Feel her loving support. All her sustenance of life is the strength and the power of her endearing support. Open your pillar of light as you imagine it going up and down your spine, connecting the earth to Source from way above. Open, soften, and receive this holy grace.

Allow these blessings to move through you. Allow the star to activate within you. See the colors now of creation enter and weave through your body, your bones, your muscles, your tissues, and each and every cell that moves through your blood. Feel the code of creation within you, now, and focus on your heart. The heart is the portal of One love. Feel it now. Breathe it in.

The star will start to spin and expand your field of light. It will extend further out, starting from your core. Further and further imagine it expands as it circles around you twelve feet more. Allow the energy of your masculine from your right to merge through. Bring it into the center and then merge it through the left side of your energy, the feminine portal of love. The two are woven together; bring the two into One. Into the center, breathe in the twin flame of love. Marry yourself fully and your star shines like the sun.

Breathe.
You are now fully anchored and firmly stabilized
and connected to Gaia and all things.
Feel this now and breathe.
Connect to all the elements and breathe in the plasmic
and stellar energies from above as they integrate
into the love codes of life here on earth.
Breathe, release, and settle into this divine pleasure of love.

You are here to resonate love, Beloveds. The message here is love. It has always been and will always be. Love, so broad, so expansive now that to capture the essence is to experience the frequencies and vibrations by releasing the lower minds pull to control.

Your journey is not unlike the journey of all souls who are seeking to find their way. You are here to master your mission and bring forth your purpose fueled within the flame. Everyone is on a journey, but yours is unique to you. No one has your signature it truly is just for you.

We take you on a journey to know deeply your true divine self. We acknowledge and affirm to you that you are more than your mind has said. Release the judgment. Allow the codes of alchemy to transform what no longer serves. The journey is allowing you to open and to receive. A space is now co-created with only your willingness. Remember to pause and bring in more.

HOW YOU VIEW THE WORLD AFFECTS ALL YOUR CHOICES

Your perception is greatly impacted by the way you perceived your world as a child and the way your needs were met by your parents and siblings. Any condition you experienced in your youth as difficult and fearful created challenges for you to trust life, yourself, and the universe around you.

However, very often, these same challenges pushed you to question your beliefs and moved you into the direction of refining where you wanted to go in life. You pondered what you wanted to create and how you choose to do it. When you broaden your view and expand your awareness, you open to allow yourself to have another reality.

Your viewpoint is made up of what is important to you. You measure your truth in relation to your beliefs. It is important for you to look at what you believe of your own nature. Who are you? What are your values? What is your connection to the world, the universe, and the energy around you? Where do these beliefs come from and do you wish to keep them? Are these beliefs serving you?

We ask you now to pause in the questions. Imagine seeing your beliefs as a garden that you cherish; sometimes you take some weeds out and other times you plant new ones. This is an ongoing process as you evolve and open your consciousness.

Everyone has a view of looking at everything. We are simply asking you to notice where your beliefs came from. Do they serve you and do you wish to keep them? Ponder in ease as you tend your garden. This will help steer your life in the direction you wish to go as it directly affects the choices you make.

Beloveds, you have forgotten the power of imagination. You have forgotten the brilliance of the child who is open to the wonder and curiosity of the world. You are the new children of the new earth. It is time to imagine instead of worrying and thinking thoughts based in fear.

Within the seed of creation lies the creative potential of all that is. To access the unlimited potential of the universe, open your imagination to create something new. Within the seeds of your creation, you may nurture it with all that you hold. We ask you to wonder why you nurture your creation seeds with worry and fright, rather than imagination and flight.

You have been programmed to believe that you must struggle and be deserving to live a life you wish or dream. All that you thought and all that you depended upon is crumbling before you. You do not have enough time,

money, support, and love. The change is now here for you
to co-create a better way, a way that is more sustaining
and forgiving of dismay. Open your hearts to imagination
and give yourself permission to experience the magic
within you. You heart starts to feel the liberation it desires
and the freedom within is manifested in all your life. New
perceptions and timelines are created on the grids of light.
Whatever you choose, you can choose again, but we ask
you to choose with openness and by cherishing your own
light. Birth a new world and co-create.

MOVING INTO YOUR CHANNEL

You are a channel, a living light portal of energy in physical
form. You have energy bodies that merge into one uniform
on this physical plane. Your body is the vehicle to ground
and embody divine light merged with the elementals of
the universal body of all that is. You hold divine wisdom
inside as the master within is waiting to uncover more gifts
that are deep within you. You are energy and you have a
physical form. What you do not see does not mean that it is
not there. The micro-waves that you are now aware of can
move faster and instantly produce heat. We are now saying
that your energy that you hold is also like this treat. As the
awareness of your scientific world expands, you uncover the
workings of the quantum land.

The flame within your heart can be ignited with your truth.
The flame will burn and produce the resurgence of your
holy divine truth. Your energy does now channel through
you, it is true, but what you choose to channel is only up
to you. The aliments in your body started in etheric form
because everything starts with energy and then manifests

into form. The awareness that you are to bring into your consciousness will enable you to detour the dis-ease within your thoughts. As a channel of holy light, you can transform it before it comes into your body and drops you to the floor. You are to manage your energy system. You are to understand that you are much more. You are to be in tune and understand your system. You are built to receive and transmit energetic signals and connect it the whole. For the World Wide Web is a symbol that brings in the broader perspective of how you are connected to all things. Open your awareness and listen to our codes. You are to connect the energies and channel abroad.

Your very nature is equipped to be the channel that you are. There is nothing special, for you were always this star. Realize the true power that you hold and consider that you do not need a special certification to be told. You are your greatest teacher if only you choose to take this road. Use discernment and go with listening to your soul. Follow the subtle energies as you stay present in the now, and as you practice this, you will develop it skillfully all around.

Others may have certain keys for you to understand, but the willingness to empower your light is for you to use with your very hands. The inter-net has given you information at your fingertips. You are now to co-create in consciousness using all the tools that are available to you to accelerate the divine plan.

Release the fear of thinking that you need to perfect more and instead experiment with co-creation and continue with your chores. All the fears you hold are common, but the common one is fear of not being good enough and your value falls on deaf ears.

There is a difference with knowing your greatness and arrogantly shouting it out loud. It is in the very resonance that you channel your energy in the now. It is in great humility that you hold within your truth that proving means that you still have doubts about the beauty of you. You are calm and stable within and you stand as a sovereign light. You channel your resonance of this holy light. You do not need the validation from others because you are sure about this instead. No longer do you look to another for the affirmation that comes from your belief that you are worthy of love and you channel this truth.

You now allow the higher light to flow. It flows through you. You think it is only for the adept and those who have gifts too. You think they are the only ones who can see beyond the veil. Yet, as you awaken to the conscious creation codes, you realize that you too have this gift and can transform all your old nodes. It will take practice. It will take presence in the light. You will need to be diligent and dedicated to the path. The use of your energy builds what you will co-create with your light. If you consciously bring intention in, you will entrain your earthly life. Everyone has intuition. It is only practice that makes you wise. Come out from under the covers and give it a try. Bring forth with great integrity that you admit that you do not know, because you know deeply you can learn what it is you need to know.

Refine your craft, we say, without any hesitation, for what is this life if you do live it fully with intention. This is a life you can live fully without fear of what others say. You are liberated and you are free to act authentically in the self you have discovered. You will continue to grow into more than you fully can comprehend. Your inventions will come into fruition as you allow others to take part in the plan, for co-creation draws from an unlimited source. Together you can achieve much greater things than what you can do on your very own. Allow the energy to flow through your channel to experience your unique gifts you are to share. Weave your consciousness with others and co-create a tapestry of love.

As you allow the flow to come through you, memories from past experiences may arise. Your internal fears of not being good enough may be your reaction and take you by surprise. You may resist expressing your power for fear you may hurt another. You may fear being different and not accepted by another. Your human nature holds fear of traveling in the unknown. You fear your future by focusing only on your past, but to consciously co-create, you must release this and embrace the present moment at last.

The only way to release fear is to walk through it and go. Close your eyes, if you must, but know you still need to go. Your willingness to stop and breathe and to calm yourself down will be the tools you need to start to chip away and anchor the divine plan. Take time if you must write down all your fears to allow them to move through you. Take time to welcome your fears and to acknowledge them by an observer from a higher perspective. Allow them to be released through the breath as you calm down. Let your body relax and your thoughts to fall away for your brain to instruct your nervous system to balance into the presence of now. The thought of danger will move away from your racing mind. Slowly bring beautiful energies of nourishment into your heart of hearts. Your channel is clearing and strengthening new filaments of light.

You are co-creating new energy and can channel more brightly your light. You are clearing your energetic filter for as you express the beliefs of your mind and your state of consciousness you can filter all the density in time. Given this, you might as well release your fears as you cannot control your channel; you can only learn to channel more of who you truly are as you change your perspective and therefore your life.

Allow the substances of the new frequencies to penetrate your fields. Open to the glory that has always been yours. Stop all the rushing. Calm yourself down. You don't need to find something. You need to BE something. Let the magic be One in you. BE the essence of love that is all. BE the miracle that is you.

Close your eyes
Breathe and smile
Imagine something you love
Let it radiate out
This is the prayer of the new world
Be diligent and manifest your heart's wish
Feel and ponder that which you are
Dance the dance
Sing the song
You are the greatness of light
Feel the wonder
Dance the wonder
Sing your wonder

What is it that you feel?

What are the senses all around you?

Feel, taste, smell
Rub your hands and focus on love
Imagine building it in your hands and fill it with
your creations
Notice your breath
Where does it go?
Taste the sweetness of life

RECONNECTION

ALIGNING THE SUBCONSCIOUS MIND TO YOUR CONSCIOUSNESS

The subconscious mind is the part of you that holds all your programs. It is like a hard drive that runs behind your conscious mind, which has stored all your past experiences.

Be curious rather than afraid.

What is love seeking to draw out of you now? In the process of co-creation, you shift in and out of love and fear. You dance between the two. Peace is present in the center point of the two. It is always there, just waiting for you. Even when the struggle takes over you, you still have the process of co-creation to tend to. Life gives you the stamina in the deliverance of your pure code. It will never take away any experience that will bring you closer to knowing the truth of yourself.

As you birth your creations and you experience the labor pains that go with it, you finally realize that it has been birthed and you are forever grateful for the creation. If only you seek to know yourself fully, for again and again the cycle will continue to shift from fear to love to peace, the only real way to know yourself is in this realm is to experience the elemental aspects of the ONE. We say to take a step back and breathe when you are tired of running, struggling, and forgetting, and bring in the sun.

Life will always be what you perceive it to be. You are only fooling yourself if you do not dismantle what you need to release. Instead, be the fool of adventure who is willing to travel within the unknown mystery. As you venture into the mystery and find your holy truth, an epiphany will come and burst through. Cry your tears of sorrow and happiness too for tomorrow is a new day and the cycle will continue.

You are moving along the tides and you get frustrated when things are hard. You wish that it would just come naturally, and you wonder how far. How do you grow, Beloveds, if not for the resistance that you come up against? Use the friction as energy to be diligent and focus on your co-creation. The friction is a signal. Stop and become aware of what is causing the tension. Do not bother to spend too much time wondering, just say a prayer to be open to something that can be positive. If you bring the willingness to see, allow yourself the time to be the witness of thee. A new perspective will be gained when you settle into your heart. Let your imagination move with the wind and the waves hold your sight. Look with soft eyes and be in the space of now. Do not worry the miracle is in the now. For a shift in your perception is truly what you seek.

Life will always happen. Things will always go this way and that. All you need to remember is to say, "Where am I at?" It is not so much a question to be answered that very moment of disdain, but instead to stop you in your tracks to pause upon the lane.

You will continue along, for your soul will always be pulsed to grow. Remember to fortify your life with love's embrace to behold. No one will be able to truly give you what you seek unless you can find it within your very own core.

Allow this time of frustration to be the awareness of it all. For all these things of happiness, and all these things of sadness, and all these things that allow ease and some pain will still bring you back to yourself within this dimensional plane.

Be well, Beloveds, and cease the moment of triumph that is right within your very core.

SAYING "NO THANK YOU, THIS IS OF MY PAST"

Recurring events from the past provide a road map for the mind when an e-motion of the same kind arises. The mind tries to identify, label it, and immediately seeks a similar sensation of an experience to find a solution to the uncomfortable e-motion that is moving through the body.

Sometimes this event becomes a recurring pattern that does not always serve you best. It is simply known to the mind because it has already been lived and embedded as it has been repeated many times. The reaction that is given by the mind pops up at the speed of light and you react in the same manner as in the past. This seems to be the solution, for you are trained to want to receive an instant result and cannot bear with the pain. Despite whether the solution is unpleasant or does not respect yourself in any way, you are conditioned to simply respond the same way because you have not created it with consciousness.

This is simply a reaction to an e-motion that is triggering you and your immediate reaction seemingly comes up to protect you, replacing the original E-motion by another that seems to be more comfortable, which very often is not to your advantage, but is known to you.

Once you start bringing awareness to your patterns, you will be able to co-create something new. By journaling your daily experience and focusing on what you considered the most challenging event of your day, you can discover what really happened and how you reacted. You also can go deeper into why you reacted in the first place, why were you triggered, and what might have frightened you or made you feel you needed protect yourself.

The first step is to see and acknowledge what you are working on. What is your daily experience trying to teach you? What is your reaction or your usual program? The more you are gently loving with yourself, releasing any judgment or guilt, the more you will be able to receive insights, day after day. You allow the unconscious patterns to reveal themselves and acknowledge ancient patterns and behaviors to come to the surface.

The next step is to ask yourself if this reaction is of service to you. Is this a win-win solution for you and those around you? Is this full of loving consciousness? You may realize that this immediate way of acting creates more and more resentment in self, more and more chaos or stress. You may experience unhappiness around you and within you. You feel as though you are moving against the grain and you are tired and are ready to change.

When you decide that your old patterns of reacting are ENOUGH and you wish to build a new reactive pattern, say, "NO thank you, this is of my past." You might even wish to add a movement of the hand to help you state this firmly, by putting your hand open in front of you to emphasize the stop. This will help you become aware of the current e-motion in your body that has been triggered through fears of the past.

By saying, "NO thank you, this is of my past," you consciously instruct your body, e-motion, mind, and soul that you are not in real danger and that you need the loving energy of comfort and support to help the parts of you that currently feel disempowered. By doing this, you co-create with your higher self, a new experience of love, forgiving the past in all the ways possible.

When you realize that you are in no immediate danger, just here and now, and by saying to yourself that it is okay to simply feel disempowered, vulnerable, or even threatened, you open to a new experience. You understand that your reaction is simply linked to a fear from the past that is coming up for resolution. This fear plays out in your energy field that was stemmed very often from the time of your childhood. It is simply a smaller part of you that is trapped in the time of the past, that is calling out to be loved, calling to be held and supported, calling out to be encouraged to release the energy of motion from the past. It has been trapped in the physical body, in the senses and in the mind that relives this past experience in the now so that it may be resolved through the power of forgiveness and love.

By acknowledging the energy in motion, the e-motion, that is traveling through your physical body and recognizing what you feel, say three times firmly, "NO thank you, this is of my past."

When you do this, you give the clear instruction to spirit that you no longer wish to react in this way. You declare that you no longer wish to cover-up an e-motion and give it power by creating more and more of it. Instead, you courageously declare to the universe that you acknowledge the wound and seek to resolve it through the power of conscious co-creation, forgiveness, grace, and love.

So, we call on you to journal an experience charged in energy. Write down the facts, the emotions that came up, and how you reacted. Observe and consider other solutions with the conscious co-creation of your higher self, you soul.

By allowing yourself to learn through the conscious observation of your daily life, you allow yourself to live a life with limitless experiences. You start to change your habits and open to a whole new level of sharing with other souls you meet every day that enable joy and love to be shared in your daily life experience. This is the access point to allow the living of your dream to be made manifest as you share your gifts consciously with all those that life brings forward.

Remember that you are co-creators of your experience and are in no way and have never been in any way powerless. Every morning, a new page of creation is gifted to you so that you may experience what you wish to co-create, what you need to learn and anchor your mastery. You gift your life with the flavor you wish to experience. All is possible, so choose to learn by acknowledging your areas of improvement and especially by recognizing all that you already achieved.

Your day's experience is limitless in time and form. It is everlasting and never ending. Decide to change what does not serve you. Choose to try something different and allow yourself to live heaven on earth by living your gift and manifesting your dreams.

Do not stay stuck in your habits. Instead, allow yourself to co-create the energy you wish to experience in your day. Carefully acknowledge your reactions that do not serve you or another, as you are the artist of your co-creation. Allow you a new draft version to be co-created and choose to consciously look at what can be improved. Go into this direction of alignment for your benefit and those all around you.

Carefully look, every evening, at all the areas of your day and notice the events where you managed a shared experience of love, support, and joy as well as any painful experience that might have been triggered by an experience that is coming up to be resolved. Take the necessary actions of change and allow yourself to have a more fulfilling life for yourself and with the others around you.

INTERCONNECTEDNESS

Open your awareness, Beloveds, and realize that everything is interconnected. Everything that you create, all our choices have an impact on your loved ones and on the entire universe. You are in a living universe that is ever evolving and is matter emerging from consciousness.

The world around you is your living library. You are here to learn through experiences. Your experiences are based on your individual perceptions and they contribute to the whole. You are here to connect with the earth and the polarities that are presented to you. This is the source energy of creation that allows a new expansion of growth.

As you connect within and through the earth's consciousness by experiencing the natural world around you, you get to entrain with the cycles of life, death, and regeneration. The code of creation is witnessed through the very currents of your earthly plane on a very visceral level of density. You have chosen to come and experience this reality to contribute to the earth's grid of light.

This grid is also connected through the galactic plane and other star systems. They too generate energy and are affected from the change that happens within Gaia. The changes that happened within the world reflect the changes that happen within your own individual consciousness. The many neurons in your body are receptors to the earth grid and your connection to her web of light, for it allows the change in your consciousness to be integrally connected as One.

The perceptions that you hold are yours. You are the master and co-creator of your reality connected to the world around you. Your very essence helps shape what you see. So, we ask you to imagine a world that can be more liberating than what you have known.

The choice to see on many planes of existence is yours and yours alone. We cannot do this for you. This is for you, for your individual code is unique to you. When your soul is driven through purpose and intention with awareness of its light, its light it can travel into the shadows and in the darkness of the polarities enabling you to experience many realities and then again, choosing what you want to co-create with the elemental fractals of the One creation.

There are many facets of creation. There are many threads of consciousness in the whole. All is part of One and One is all. What we are here to remind you is that your discovery is your gain. So, open to the internal wisdom that your heart is sure to ignite within the flame. As the fire burns inside you to light the darkest fright away, remember that the waters have been your origin and it will masterfully adapt to the change.

Flow with the waters after you have burned your sorrow away. Come back to the essence of your brilliance and allow all troubles to float away.

What will manifest or be created into denser form will be what is in the physical for all to be adorned.

Create with love and love will be created. A new form of love will grow within the code of co-creation. We are One. We are All.

WHEN ALL SEEMS WRONG

When you complain and focus on what is wrong, you create more of it and continue to magnetize more. You tell all your friends and coworkers too, how hard it is for them as well as it is for you. If only they would do this or do that, things will be better just like that! Your frustration builds and you are ready to explode. Yet you do not realize, dear heart, that you are creating the drama in the show.

The plot thickens and the hostilities begin to rise. There is envy, jealously, and tensions run high. You say that you do not have enough; you are suffering and are in pain. You say you are tired; you need to leave and walk away. Your friends do hear you and discuss more of the same. You say that this is not for you and you cannot take it anymore! The day does end, and you go about it once more. It is another day as you created more you continue to blame another, and you get say it is a chore.

The cycle continues. On and on it does go, until one is willing to strengthen the vision that they hold. Yet, the vision is impossible your friends may say. You discuss it, analyze it, and exchange feelings and are afraid that if you left this situation today, what will then happen, and how will you make your way? You do not think it is possible to live your wishes and your dreams. You are disappointed in the life you live and criticize and judge that you were never worthy of anything anyway. You forget it for now and do it another day. Yet, the feelings of defeat, abuse, and neglect continue to fester. You create dis-ease in your body and cannot lift a finger.

Beloveds, do not live in the future or in the past. Live in the present and gain great access to your liberation at last. Pass all the suffering that you have agreed that you must bear. Transform your life by seeing the magician in the mirror. Be the alchemist and change the figures. It will call on your wisdom and your inner eye. It will ask you to follow the alignment of your heart and third eye. You will embark on a journey of co-creative abilities to build a new world full of strength and nobility.

Learn the lessons that your soul is teaching thee that you can be the master co-creator of the life you dream. There are many ways to react. It will come down to two things: you either live it or believe or believe it and live it. The choice is yours. You get to believe.

Remember that the future does not exist yet. It has yet to come. So, all is possible and the energy you give it will co-create in the perfect now. It will impact today, bringing it into tomorrow. It will affect all your friends and you will model a leader of a new tomorrow. You will encourage others with the new vision that you hold instead of staying in the same old energy of complaining and feeling old.

Choose to use your energy wisely and focus on what you want to create, rather than focusing on the life that you hate. What crosses your field is a mirror of what is inside. If you are triggered and want to react to the anger that is built up inside, the emotions need to be released. Forgiveness lends its hands to allow you the time it is needed to realize this new truth, for the soul is always learning and pulsing to find its truth.

Simply breathe and acknowledge the fear and of holding much doubt. Release it if you do not wish to recreate the past. Come into the wisdom of the unknown mystery. Ride the waves of deliverance and bring forth your new creations that are filled with great potentially.

Prepare for more possible outcomes. Prepare to meet the lover, the giver, and the receiver of pure divine gold.

Everything remains possible and all can miraculously be betrothed in the christed light. Call on the assistance of Mother Gaia and spirit to assist you through the realm of magic through and through.

CO-CREATION—The Song of the Star

Imagine this code assisting you to open to unity consciousness. Allow it to connect you with your star families and open you to the many pathways of wisdom. Connect deeply with all aspects of yourself as you gaze at this code. Imagine and ponder the wisdom you have gained throughout your journey as you traveled through the portals of creation. Remember your essence and see yourself in the cosmos traveling and birthing through the many levels of consciousness and beyond.

Consider that this experience is gifting you far beyond what you could ever imagine. You will know from the bottom of your heart that this is your truth, no matter how impossible it may seem to your human mind. Reconnect with your divine nature, to your cosmic essence. By doing so, you will encounter the powerful creator that you are as you experience profound gratitude for this extraordinary, multidimensional experience.

CHAPTER 6

CO-CREATION THE SONG OF THE STARS

Beloveds,

The song of the star is within you, deep within the core of you. When the star spins and is ignited, it resonates the code of you. The sound rings your unlimited potential that is accessed in the silence of everlasting love. It sings it out for all to hear feel and know.

Hold the note, the frequency that raises you to the stellar levels of light. Hold the code; for the code of light starts to move through your channels for your portal to expand into other dimensions that then create ripples of violet light. For the ripples do come from the center and then out, reverberating the sound of One heart light. For all is together in the One heart of light. Together we will discover the many facets of colors that weave all together that create a story of light. And as the light is now shed, and the blanket is created, the woven pieces of love become a bond of light.

I no longer follow the old ways I have known
I no longer travel into judgment and pain
I see all the colors
Everything I created

I bless all these cycles and lift from a new place
I recreate a pattern
Spinning around and round me
I know that I will be baffled
By all the light codes I have traveled
I am now, I am
I am
I am
I am now, I am
I am
I am home
I let the new threads spin
Around the old threads
Into the One heart now
All does merge in time
Something new emerges
Out of spinning spirals
In the magic of no time
I create a new day as the spirals sound
Sound my new love
Sound the presence of now
Sound a new way
Sound the presence of now
I breathe in this moment
Let all my thoughts go
I hear the music
that plays within my soul
It is singing
It is singing
Home, home, home
It is spinning
It is spinning

Round and round
Everything is moving
As I shine my light now
Weaving threading turning all the sounds of love
Round and round the spiral sounds with the magic of love
Round and round the spiral sounds with the magic of love
Oh, oh, oh, oh
Let the bells chime now
Sparkling down the light specs
All the angels come now
And surround you with love
Open and receive now
The very blessings
They have always known that life spirals do unfold
All we really need to know
Is that movement happens TO and FRO
It is never-ending spirals
Will always turn into it
to discover more of the self
Oh, oh, oh, oh
Stop waiting for another
And come into the center
All is well and you can tell
The story of One love for the self
Open and receive now the grace of light that shines upon
Do you feel our love now?
Pouring through your crown

We come to you now Beloveds to speak to you regarding
miracles. A word that is used so commonly and yet one
does not really know the magnitude of what is possible or
the potentiality of allowing the flow of the universe to take
hold in your life.

So, we say the paradox is here and we will explain. Miracles are common, for they happen as you co-create your life whether with consciousness or not, for it is the natural flow of life. To notice the miracles awareness is born in the presence of the moments that unfold. These moments create experiences you encounter in your life. Miracles are synonymous with pure gratitude, for when one leaves judgment and expectation behind, the miracles of life become the forefront of one's consciousness.

We tell you to look for the miracles in the everyday. It means to take all of life as a pure gift for the essence that it is. And yet, as we explain the commonality of this experience, we want to bring you the awareness of the profound nature of what this means as well. For all these things that you never imagined in your life has happened and you could not have anticipated where the path has led you to, that, my dear, is a miracle. When you realize this, you are starting to understand the code of creation.

When your inner truth comes into alignment with the deepest part of your essence, you will begin to realize that everything you create with Divine light consciousness is a miracle. You will create the energetic patterning of conscious manifestation of miracles.

So, the spiral does now turn again, and you come back around with an explanation of what a miracle truly is, but we say to you that pure experience of the miracle is the subtle nuance of your energetic field and your physical body in form coming together in the marrying of wholeness.

This alchemic stream becomes the flow of life everlasting to touch many potentialities that are specific to your individual soul's code of life. Thus, setting up the pattern of miraculous events that can unfold because you allow the flow to be part of you, and you experience the joy of living life. From your heart center where compassion resides, you can send out beams of light that only has one intention, the intention of love. Love, a state of being that has no attachment or conditions, only love.

SUCCESS

OPENING TO SUCCESS

Living in equanimity is key.

When you harness the mind and the body, keeping everything in balance within yourself, you open your mind to receive inspiration. You are in phase with the Universe as you pay attention to what life brings forth to you. You are then able to see what others do not see and hear what others do not hear.

By keeping a good level of energy within you, you create an excess of energy that allows you to face what life brings to you. You will have energy to respond. You will be passionate about life and attract more and more of the same toward you.

It is important that you are conscious of what you are offering to the field around you. What are you proving to yourself and others, as each one of you is participating in the dance of the collective experience?

Creating through integrity and having the intention to
stay of conscious as you act for the good of all will create
a field of trustfulness around you that will enhance deeply
your success.

What is success?
What brings you joy?
What are you opening to?
What will be in store?
Everything is a magical field of all your wishes and dreams
If only you ensure within that the magic indeed is within
Be here now Open to your light
Be here now Ground into the light
You bring in many colors
And master codes of love
Be here now
And revel in the unknown
Success is all part of this
The discovery of the light
How you measure
Who is to say?
Just open to your light
Your heart is willing to receive
Once it lets go of what is thinks it knows
The mystery brings forth more of which
Is the master generator of the nodes
Success is yours
When you bring forth your light
Churn it and twirl it with your might
And send it out to flight
The only way it can fly
Is when you can open and receive
For the heart's greatest,

greatest gift
Is to be able to open to its gifts!

HOW TO AVOID CREATING BLOCKS

When you feel angry or hurt, your body contracts. You then enter a defensive mode that was conditioned in your being when you were a child.

This will, of course, be different for everyone, either becoming passive by fleeing and not saying what you really want to say, or by entering conflict by shouting and trying to hurt the other like you were hurt.

These situations inevitably appear even when you are conscious of the way you feel and react. And why is that? It is because life is making you grow, day after day. This journey is the path of healing. It is an exploration of your memories from childhood into how you respond as an adult.

Therefore, you often see similar patterns between parents and children through the family linage. The way of interacting with each other and the ways of speaking and behaving are a certain signature for the family.

Life is the opportunity to understand how you react when you are hurt and when you feel that things are unsafe and unfair. When you feel unsafe inside, process what is really taking place by simply observing without judgment. Be curious and wonder what life is asking you to heal and release.

Your ego will want to define the situation, analyze, and deduct a reason and solution. Take time for it to express all it wants to say, but do not share with another, say it out loud with nobody to listen to you except you. Let your ego speak. This is the first step in co-creating with your ego. Take all the time you need to cool off.

After some time, do not stay too long; know that this is only the first step of the process and you can decide that now is the time for you to start the healing.

1. Sit down or lie down comfortably and start breathing. Concentrate on your breath. The deeper you go, the slower the in breath and out breath. The more you will calm down and your ego will be able to loosen up a bit. You will slowly but surely step out of the event that triggered you.

2. After some time, you will feel more peaceful. This will allow you to distance yourself or detach from the situation that triggered you and made you react in a certain way.

3. Take the time now for reflection. What is happening inside of you? Do not focus on how you lived the chaotic situation or how you reacted. Simply notice what is going on inside of you. What was triggered inside you? When did you get hurt and did not say anything, and, from this point on, were you in fact in reaction mode?

Take the time in the moment of the experience to assess when you are hurt. This will facilitate the transformation as you harness the energies of the present moment. Pause into the moment. Often, the situation may be a minor event when another is unaware and does not intend to hurt you, for they too are in their unconscious conditioning.

If you can allow yourself to be present, tend to the wound, and deal with you in the present moment, you will be able to efficiently manage your energy system. You no longer need to transform your past experiences as you are in the present co-creating your life.

1. The healing comes by taking this wounded part of you in your arms with your full attention and support like you would take care of a wounded child, through the power of your heart. You do not need to understand how you made this your protection mode. You do not even need to go back into your past. Do not get lost in the semantics, fuel it with more power and analyze it which would makes it more difficult to decipher. All you need to do is comfort, release, and restore the love that you thought you did not have in that moment.

2. It is through feeling the vibration of love and allowing the contracted energy to release through the bliss of universal love that you will be able to dissolve the memory of the wound that is stored inside. This is an opportunity for you to let go and for-give.

3. Choose to make your well-being your priority. Assist yourself by allowing your mind and ego to relax as they have rung the bell to alarm you that a part of you was suffering. Build the strength within to self-comfort. You can do so even if you were not taught this as a child. As you draw in more of your light from your higher self, you can fulfill your own needs. No longer do you look to another to give you what you need from feelings of lack. Conscious co-creation is working with others in pure sovereignty as each lives the gift they are inspired to share. It does not create

from lack, but rather from celebration and the pulsing of one's creative passion within.

4. Make your inner well-being your priority. Stop and address your wounded selves as soon as they appear. Do not let your wounds call in your ego to protect you and your mind to find a solution; instead, call on your higher self for assistance. Stay in your body. Open your heart to yourself. Breathe and bring love unto you.

5. Thank life for the teaching and the opportunity to transform the old. Realize with gratitude that your healing process is a gift to yourself and humanity, as you will create much less drama and chaos. By making your healing your main priority, you gift yourself and others and allow all those around you to do the same.

WHAT IS THE PURPOSE OF YOUR HUMAN SELF?

Your human cannot figure out the mystery of the light in the unseen. That is why it is called a mystery. This is something beyond the veil, but still has great power. Your power of co-creation will rely on your ability to sense and intuit your energy field. For your human body is the vehicle of your soul. Your soul is vast and comes from pure consciousness. It has no limits as it has no form.

Your human self is responsible for the choices you make. This is your free will. This is, in fact, HUGE. Your physical body is the channel to which all higher frequencies of love and light can come through. It can ground the energies and allow it to affect the natural world too. It can allow transformation to occur within and through the realms of spirit as well in the realms of physical form.

To retrieve your true nature of pure innocence and infinite creative potential, open yourself to love and be grateful for your human body and the human part of you that is in denser form, which includes lower vibrations of doubt and fear. It was written that all will be transformed from the density to achieve a greater acceleration of evolution throughout the cosmos. It is and continues to be a great experiment for all.

By allowing the master within to live in your daily experience you can integrate the master that you are on this earthly world. You bridge heaven and earth and allow wholeness to be once more. Being in oneness does not mean that you will all choose the same thing; you will choose what is appropriate for you according to your essence. Oneness means that you are part of the whole, but your individuation contributes to streams of light and consciousness that enables the expression of creation source to be more of what it is.

It is only you who can choose to open to the divine perfection that is coded within you. Your Master within awaits your calling. By judging and shunning the parts of you that you do not accept, you limit your elevation into higher consciousness as it is through the embracing of your human experience that you will understand that consciousness moves energy into form, creating your reality.

Experience this moment where you are completely present realizing that you are not only human, but also divine as a master co-creator of your life. You are whole. You can sit in the moment and realize that you are the human having the experience with the master that is assisting you. It is time for you to experience growth without pain, life without struggle. Open to this possibility!

Treat your human self with respect, gentleness, and loving care. If you stress or struggle, ask yourself, "Why do I want this?" You might be surprised with the level of consciousness that is present.

We invite you to LOVE yourself with the most love you could give another. Practice this as it will open you to another level of consciousness and integrate with higher parts of you more and more every day.

Beloveds, you are here to experience yourself in human form to co-create new seeds of higher light in physical form. More codes of light are coming through your earthly plane to evolve into the galaxy and with the family of stars. Your human form has a masterful way of adapting to higher light codes. It has been seeded from long ago to awaken and birth the divine plan.

You have always known when your consciousness was light, that you would deliver on a day that has earth, air, waters, fire, and higher light, for the frequencies on your planet are changing and transforming into a higher octave of light. Your bodies carry within it too the en-codement of this higher light. How else were you to anchor this and seed it and watch it grow? You are here to nourish it and experience the beauty and bliss. It is not just your humanness that you are contributing to, but the universe's as a whole.

You think the angels are better than you because they are wiser and of the light, but believe it when we say to you that they are looking to you to anchor much lighter, for they too need to evolve because they are consciousness of light.

One is not better than the other, but all must be honored on this plane. The grass is not greener somewhere else when you are the master of your play. Stand in the green grass of fruitful pastures and allow co-creation to fulfill your homes. Feel the abundance of loveliness and celebrate this joy.

MOTIVATION

LIVING THE EXPERIENCE FULLY— IT IS NEVER TOO LATE

You are busy working, speaking, walking, doing, and going on your way. Are you fully engaged and experiencing the play? The time keeps on ticking, you never have enough, but what we are saying, Beloveds, is that there is enough. Time is yet an illusion and the busyness of the day does not mean that you get where you want to go in constant action day to day. To fully appreciate and live in the experience fully is the epic task of the day. Be the stillness in the motion and practice this day to day. It will allow you to bypass the pain and head for the flowers to smell the sweetness of the day. Trust in the rightness of the moment if you are to move or stay. Be present in your knowing because what is yours cannot be taken away. When being in the non-doing, your senses are magnified. The intensity of the experience is surely multiplied. Allow the expansion of living to become more vibrant and alive. Live in the essence and your voice will arise.

This is a skill to be exercised as you have dulled all your senses for fear of the unknown. Enter the brilliance of this feeling of being alive by being fully present in the moment. Expand the perfection of the experience by settling into the breath. Even if you have the impression that rushing throughout life gives meaning to all your craziness that you are not willing to admit. The collective says that this is righteous and do not dare to quit.

When you step out of the chaos and witness what your life has become, you may want to slow down to transform what unconsciously was done. Bring forth creative consciousness into the forefront of your life and feel fully the sensation of the experience you confront.

Exercise the sensations and experiment with the now. Be willing to drop into the body and listen with a full heart. You will learn to differentiate an emotion from the portal of the heart that has all the knowing without the physical show or the taste of what is tart.

Your heart will expand, and grace will come forth. You will be thankful for the experience that life has brought. Remember that at any given moment, you can slow down. Even when you are ready to sleep, you can feel the present moment in your bed. Feel the intensity of your energy when you focus on it with full intent.

By taking a moment to expand your senses, you nourish your body, mind, and spirit. This provides a wondrous flavor to your experience into the heart of now. Enjoy what really happens as you make the most of the moment. Expanding your heart fully has an expression of your day.

By doing so, you will release the impression of not really living your life, for it is through the sensing of it that you make the most of all the blessings that come your way. All the sharing of love with another can be savored and enjoyed. This simple process of living each experience fully can change your perception of what is. Miracles are a change of perception and you open to this each day.

Life is a precious gift and time stands still as all seems to be. Take the moments in preciousness and witness the sensing of love. The moment gives you many things if you remain still in the busyness of all things. Listen to what others say deeply from within. Be present with what comes up as your feelings move like the wind. The hummingbird has much to say in the presence of its flight. It flits about very joyfully as it stays in one spot. Be the joy of love again in the fullness of your breath. It will always bring you back into the beauty of the moment if you let it.

Feel the vibration of the experience!

CHOOSING TO BRING JOY INTO YOUR EXISTENCE

When you practice conscious co-creation and bring into your life what you truly desire, you realize that what you have been searching for has always been within you. Joy fills you as you embody this knowing. You discover that all comes from within.

Exercise gratitude to bring more of what you truly want in your life. Focus your energy on what energy you wish to share. Disconnect from the habit of activating feelings and thoughts of lack. Give new instructions to the universe and you shall receive in return what you were craving for.

Through this practice, you will discover that you have less and less preferences, as when you put space around you and surrender, you receive so much more, far beyond what you could have imagined. Your ideas do not come anymore from your brain, but from your enlightened soul. You know profoundly and follow the guidance. This inspiration moves through your consciousness because you have opened to receive through the space around you, emptied the mind, and elevated your vibration in the field of the universal consciousness.

Beloveds, go, walk, and trod to better horizons. Into the sun, out of the sun—it makes no difference, for the light of day is within your soul. Within the heart of hearts, into the magic you will go. Into the bliss of forever expanding cosmos all on the traces of time until you bounce and skip along the pebbles of time.

Each one you feel, hear, and know, further and further you will go, into and onto the spirals of all of eternity. For this spiral will never stop. You will always grow to be love. All you really need is love for yourself and to share with others.

Catch the music on the wind. Put it in your heart. Find the grace between the space and dance, dance, dance on the wings of change.

FOCUS ON BEING THE EXPRESSION OF YOUR SOUL

We invite you to be the divine expression of your soul. To choose this path, it will take your engagement and determination. We are here to assist you as you unfold through the mystery. The more you partner with the divine, the more you allow the master blueprint of your divinity to come forth. The master plan is to embody and choose from divine will that is unique to your path. You are the sacred expression of the love and wisdom of your soul.

Accept every moment and surrender to all that comes to you with the willingness to learn something new. As you accept life, blessings can be received and you will be able to anchor more and more light, becoming a divine wisdom channel.

When you bestow a blessing, it does not mean you agree, nor that you want more, it allows you to recognize that there is a higher plan and that you trust that all has a purpose. Each time you send love or give a blessing, you neutralize negative karma. However, your cells know when things are true or not; this blessing needs to come from your heart, even if your heart feels broken. Your ego might give you all the reasons why not to bless; you need to process your ego, as if you do not forgive, it will create karma and the cycle will continue.

Your journey is to love everything unconditionally. A blessing can only come through love. When you are aligned to divine will, you have surrendered to the universe and the universe surrenders to you. Surrendering is the energy of flow and the anchoring of divine will upon this earth.

Nevertheless, healthy boundaries are particularly important. If someone has stolen from you, you are upset and know that they are taking a part of your karma. When you feel resentful, choose to forgive so that you do not need to bring them back into your life. Bless them and accept your learning through this experience in life, opening to a greater discernment, realizing through this experience of life that boundaries are good for you.

Your throat chakra holds the master blueprint of your soul and your physical body. It connects you to your divine perfection. It holds the universal records and gives access to the vastness that has made you who and why you are what you are. You are on the path of divine expression to become the voice of your soul. This is a big initiation, taking time to refine, as it is your power of creation. Learn to speak impeccable words and tones to create what you really want through the power of your heart and not through the wounds of your emotions nor the limited beliefs of your ego.

We invite you to be conscious of what are you saying to yourself. Look in front of a mirror and ponder if you instantly judge others when you see them. Does your initial reaction come from a place of love? If you have an instant program of judgment, acknowledge it, do not judge yourself even more, as when you do so, you return through this internal spiral of judgment. Acknowledge it. Ask your soul to help you see every time you act out this destructive habit. Choose to return to your heart and apologize. Send blessings to you or another.

Use this powerful tool of instantly saying the word, DISCREATE. Say it out loud to use the power of the word to consciously choose to discreate a form, an expression, or an action, which will dissolve all to make sure only love remains and allow you to step out of creating the negative karmic pattern of judgment.

It is important to honor the words that come through. Consciously choose them and make sure your words come from a place of love and are centered in the wisdom of your heart. By connecting your throat chakra with your heart chakra, you will allow every part of your being to be supported with a greater level of love in your life. Ask yourself, is this for my benefit or the benefit of others? Am I reacting or responding? What is your intention of saying what you are saying?

When you start going beyond your imbalanced expression, may this be through words, movement, action, the way you dress, how you eat, or all those habits that you took on and that do not define the truth of your soul's essence, you will encounter your own originality and your essence, which deepens the expression of your soul. Your divine intention is to co-create through love and wisdom, being heart-full, seeing how your words affect others, as you cannot take them back. Speak with humility and selflessness, with the intention of having the most impeccable pure expression of love and wisdom.

Beloveds, you are a light being. You have been created through the light of creation. The many aspects of you are the creation codes of multi-universes that live inside of you. To experience more of yourself through love, the more you will experience the enfoldment of your true nature.

The journey of finding your essence time and time again is the beauty of discovering you. You have many possibilities, many opportunities to find out more about you through the way you relate with others, through the way you see the natural world around you, and through the way you hold yourself in the eyes of love and compassion.

All these opportunities are here for you. You are abundantly given this opportunity time and time again, if only you see your life as a discovery instead of feeling trapped in victim consciousness. Your physical world will align with your spiritual work as you practice and fortify these new codes of creation within you. Trust and know that there is much happening behind the scenes and continue your path of discovery.

Creation is a wonder and to birth a new world, one needs the willingness to believe in love instead of fear. You have struggled and felt much pain in your world. The time of freedom, love, and ease is here for you as you balance the energies within you. This is the mastery that we talk about, the ability to balance the polarities within you; as you unify your field of light you balance the many aspects of you into the master co-creator of the new.

CREATIVITY

OPEN TO RECEIVE

Beloved One, you are not alone. In the process of the seeding your dream, when the form is unknown, as the dream is at its beginning, understand that we are here to assist you.

Choose to open your heart to our loving support. Choose to consciously call on our presence by your side.

This is for you to decide, as you are the master of your creation. As you are a co-creator, you create together with the support of Mother Earth and the Universal consciousness. When creating a dream that is for the good of all, that is yet unknown to you in its final form, consciously working hand in hand with the full support from spirit is key.

The bigger the project, the more support you will need, so take time to call in the help that you need. When doing so, the entire universe surrounds you and organizes itself around your profound desire.

So, take time to slow down your rhythm, allow the breath of life to come in and nourish you with its caresses. Feel the embrace of the loving support of what is called the invisible world. Let yourself be held in a loving embrace. Instruct each of your cells to be infused with love. Feel it. Sense it. Know it. Allow the experience for love to fully enter your life. Know that you are not alone in this seeding process and that Spirit already knows the outcome of all this creation for the good of all.

Take time to just sit and receive the love of the Mothers, these conscious beings that have undertaken the mastery of birthing. Surrender to the form and allow them to assist you, to nourish you, to hold you and love you. Feel it. We are here.

Sit in silence, breathe, and receive!

Breathe into the code of love with us as we connect our hearts as One. Allow the remembrance of your pure divine essence to circulate throughout your field in love. Relax your body and let go of the tensions, for the contractions are moving through you. You are feeling the contractions of birthing anew. But we say to you as you birth this new version of you, that you can now let go the belief that the contractions need to be painful. Only see them as more of an opening rather a struggle, confusion, or fear. Come into the knowing that this birthing process is happening, and you can go with the flow of it with ease and grace as you allow the rhythms and cycles to move through you. Each space holding, releasing in and out again, is the cycle of contracting and expanding within you.

The code of love is here to offer the support when it is needed. The awareness to open to it is key. So instead of doing the labor on your own, open to receive this divine grace. This is the opening for a stream of miracles, a stream of new consciousness to fill you.

Connect fully with Gaia. Connect fully with your star within. Connect fully with the grace from Source and the Divine of All That Is.

Sit with us and receive this grace and breathe.

You have heard the call and you are listening. You are now choosing within the trust and fortification of your divine true nature. You are bringing in the code of your majesty. You are feeling and knowing your true worth and your unique gifts that are to be shared with others. You are falling in love with you. Quiet times are reflective times as the wind does blow onto you. You hear the trees, you watch the waters, the mountains do stand firmly for these elements to come into place as you come into the center of the One heart space.

We have always been with you, Beloved, and trust and faith are at the cornerstone of this next journey, for you are at the gateway of discovering the truth and purpose of all that your hold. No longer are you to vanish away in judgment and in doubt, for that time is erased and a new upgrade will come into your existence.

We ask you to follow a path that leads to an opening of new life. There will be many options and portals, but you will be guided.

So, listen now to the silence of your desires, Dear One, for they are the clues to your deliverance. No longer shall you shun your majesty away in the dark for we will sing the songs of love into the vastness of the ocean and in the mountains as we bring forth the energetic codes of revelation and purification. We are here to assist you to discover and bring forth magic into your life full of stories that are a part of your divine nature. All is well. Do not force. Just be.

We are here to help you access the essence of grace and to allow these energies to flow through you. For the resonance of grace can be experienced in this now moment and acclimate into your frequency and vibration.

First, call on the Angel of Grace. Breathe in this life force of love as the essence of grace starts to filter through. Grace weaves through all aspects of you. You begin to become aware of the truth of you, that you are love in pure essence. This awareness is a step into the co-creation of your true self. Feel the love and light that you are as the streams of grace fill your column of light, as we embrace all parts of you, the parts that are in fear and doubt as well as the parts that hold the gifts of the Beloved within you. This is your star of creation that is within your heart. All of grace starts to merge with the sun and moon into One heart. All does now blend into this ever now moment as we honor the existence of all things into the heart of love.

When grace fills you, judgment falls away and the love brings you through the path of the heart. This portal of love can resonate at a higher rate to arise from the density and darkness as an alchemic process of love transforms back into One. Light and dark do now become One and into a new resonance of the rebirth and higher consciousness.

Grace allows wisdom into your senses and widens your perception. To see within the frequency of grace is the establishment of the core place of love.

So now, we weave grace through again and again as the cycle does turns, as the spiral does turn, spin around and around and back again.

Open now and receive the grace of light and move with the confidence that the past is now done and the new is created right before you. Co-creation codes merged with stellar codes of love will now ring in the brilliance of the star above, below and within. The star now comes forth blooming and opening to the rays of light and love. Grace is now yours.

CYCLES OF CREATION

All creations are made of a spiral, ongoing evolution, uplifting if you let it do so, or repeating if you still need more of what was.

Notice and observe in what cycle you are. Is it time for you to sit and open to receive the dream? Is it time for you to seed, nourish, or harvest?

Nothing can be rushed; the phase of the cycle is very important for you to notice because life is blissful when you are aligned to the flow and in phase with the cycle of creation that is present.

The phase of sitting still to receive the guidance, without wanting or needing anything, is most probably the most difficult one. However, it is the most important phase as you can start new, fresh, and innovate as you are in the phase of the dream. What is required of you is to do nothing, to not think, not feel, not move, it is for you to open to your awareness and your highest potential. It is the time of knowing deeply that creation will use your gifts in the most optimal way. It will allow your creativity to pour through and inspire you. By sitting and waiting to be guided, you open to all possibilities and activate your creativity, which will ease the next phase of seeding, nourishing, and harvesting.

Beloveds, we ask you to call in the passion that comes deep within you. We ask you to ignite the fire within to fuel your passion through and through. We ask you to discover what makes you curious, what sparks your attention, and from that vantage point, continue the journey of discovery. Passion comes from the force of life that wants to discover and rediscover itself in many forms, facets, nuances, and the like. You were never meant to stay in one form, in one place, or in one energy. Growth is the law of the expansion. It will always happen whether you choose it or not. The soul will always seek to know more of itself. In the cycles of creation, the discovery is the trick. Discovery is the rise of the passion within. When one is in his or her passion— compassion leads the way. For you no longer need to defend what you know it to be and will always be in the end, and yes in the beginning.

So, call in passion. Come Passion! Come Passion! Come be my guiding light. Come Passion! Help me discover my truest and brightest light.

THE MORE PROGRAMS DISSOLVED, THE MORE YOU MANIFEST ALL THAT YOU ARE

You have experienced your creations being birthed through your conditioning of the past, the programming of your DNA through past experiences that have be relived over and over again, reimprinting your childhood. This has often created what you did not want or dream of.

You have chosen to learn and spent time releasing, healing, and dissolving the roots of your deep programming on all levels. You have experienced taking a moment to choose to stop when you find yourself spiraling down, to tune into your heart, and connect to infinite gratitude. To prevent the downward spiral, observe your overwhelming emotions and fears. Do not to deny them, as you will need to take time to see why you created this as your reality.

Deep gratitude is a creative energy. When you call it, feel it, and practice it, it allows you to drop into the depth of that vibration. As you radiate vibrations of compassion and love, you attract situations and people that resonate at that level.

When choosing to live through the radiance of your understanding and inner wisdom, you become better at attracting more of what you dream of, manifesting more of what you want, crystalizing with high vibrations and intentions, and initiating immediate creation.

Beloveds, quiet yourself to listen and feel what you truly love. Quiet yourself to listen and hear the whispers of your soul. Quiet yourself to listen and watch the seed grow.

It is time to nurture that which you want to see grow and tend to your very being. Your center is this calming place to stop, watch, and listen. Do you hear the callings of your soul? Ask and know all guidance will be given unto thee. It will be to those who are willing to seek. Stop, look, and listen. Hear the grumblings and feed your soul.

The expansion is here, and the contraction is here. The dance between the two is the balance. The only way to balance is through the dance. So, dance, dance, dance!

ABUNDANCE

OPENING TO THE SPACE WITHIN

When you take time to just dance with the music, close your eyes for your body to move as it wants. Allow the movement to release all tensions. You might even want to tap with your hand on the constricted parts of your body, waking up those parts of you as you dance. You can also roll on the floor, shake your body, and much more. Just allow yourself to be creative and enable your body to release through the sound of music and the dancing of the body.

When you feel that your body has been satisfied, heard, and can now open to more space within, stop and lie down.

Calmly relax your body and place all your attention on your breath while you push out from your belly. Fill your left leg with the breath. With the outbreath, release all that can be released. Do the same with the other leg, and now both legs.

Breathe in through your all the region of your belly, in front and through your back. Fill this region with air and release. Do the same with your abdomen. Fill in your heart space in front and behind, then release.

Do the same with your throat and your shoulders. Bring the breath to your brain and skull. Breathe in the air from your feet to the top of your head, a bit like a wave of breath. Use the air to bring more space in your body.

Fill your skin with the breath and enliven your entire body. Allow more space within.

This simple exercise will allow you to expand and move density out of the body. It will nourish and provide healing energies to realize your emotional and mental tensions that are stored in your body. You might even wish to expand the breathing beyond your physical body into your aura, allowing more space into your existence. Be well, Beloveds. Breathe.

CO-CREATION WITH THE UNIVERSAL LAWS

Beloved, we come to you this day to remind you that you are connected throughout the mystery of the universe. Nothing is impossible, nothing is unreachable, and nothing cannot be created if you respect the Universal laws. The basis of life is that all tends to return to balance. If chaos is created, it will return to its original source energy, which is balance.

As you experience this planet earth, you have been given the gift of free will. This is so as you are here to learn how to master your creations. You can create from an ego perspective, which will always want to prove itself right and create separation, as it has no consciousness of being collectively connected with all other creation beings. These creations are mostly unbalanced, as they most often come from a space of fear, lack, and suffering creating what is called karmic debts. As all is bound to come back to balance, you will at a certain point be driven by life in some difficult situations not understanding why all this is happening to you.

All in existence has its purpose, nothing is useless, and you need to accept that most often you do not understand why it is. Life will bring challenges to you to learn how to co-create in a balanced way. This will enable you to grow as you are all on the path of evolution.

By becoming conscious that you are One of the whole, you realize that you are connected to all sentient beings on this planet and to Mother Nature. Your creations will automatically impact the whole and you will start to make sure that your choices that generate your thoughts, feelings, and actions are aligned to the good of all.

In this process of growing up, you will heal, expand your consciousness, and open profoundly your heart. Allowing you to grow emotionally, mentally, physically, and spiritually. This is the path of evolution that is asked of every human being; to become conscious of your thoughts, feelings, and actions that impact the whole. Knowing that it is together that you will be able to change this world and allow more love to sit in your human experience.

Every action has a repercussion. Every choice has an effect. You seem to think that things just happen to you without realizing that everything you do affects the whole. In this collective consciousness that we share, we get to see our thoughts, beliefs, and feelings manifest in form for the whole.

Yes, we say we, for even consciousness not in form is connected to the whole. Therefore, we are here to bring forth the messages of love to you. It is because it affects our evolutionary process too. We have come and will always connect to those who choose to connect in ways expansive to what seems to be nothing at all.

Our consciousness connects to yours and we can create a new collective consciousness as we bring in the higher light frequencies and expand your codes of creation into something more. What you have experienced so far is part of the cycle of evolution. We are now asking you to revolutionize the way you have done things and begin another cycle of creation that is more expansive, more inventive than before.

Many have believed that their thoughts and ideas were not enough, and you rely solely on those who have more access to your monetary wealth to lead the way. But in a great time of change and crisis, those that you looked to you for guidance is now becoming clearer and clearer that the attitudes they hold are not necessarily the attitude that is good for the whole.

Throughout these times of struggle and pain, many have only done things for their own personal gain because they feared that there would not be enough or have enough access to the star stuff. But we say to you, Beloveds, that this is not the truth. The truth is that the universe and the planes of consciousness beyond are much more abundant than what you have felt as unkind.

It is time to create a new story of what can be told that is filled with expansion as you let go the old. The old ways of seeing are truly stagnant we say, for your ability to create has much more in the play.

ABUNDANCE AND MONEY

Abundance is at all levels, the richness of the heart, of love, of power of money, all are linked.

Money is not a goal in itself; it is in service in this world to live properly. You cannot do anything without money. When you earn money, it is for you and all the others around you. Be mindful with an open heart as you send it to others and onto yourself.

Some people do not feel worthy enough to ask to receive money or abundance because their ego holds beliefs of shame, and this creates major difficulties in their lives. Some are not conscious to heal these wounds, which create dramatic situations in their lives. Others like to be assisted and do not want to become powerful creators and some are scared to lose what they have. In all cases, it is the ego that hangs on to limitations to prevent you from having what you dream of.

All is a question of balance in the giving and receiving for self and others. If you only give, you slave away and if you only receive, you store. All loses its use and stagnates. It is the same with money. You earn it then save it to share in service for you and your loved ones and more when possible. You can become sick when giving too much or receiving too much without sharing.

If you look closely, your refusal to have money is in fact a refusal to be free; it is a fear of your limitless true nature. Keeping a balance is important, as when you gather too much money, you are finally not free anymore either.

Money is intimately spiritual, as it allows you to practice the energy of giving and receiving. Money is a unit of measurement. It is not the source of unlimited creative potential. Realign your mastery of conscious co-creation and use the situations in your life as opportunities to practice giving and receiving in balance. As a child you were taught to share. You were taught that to maintain harmony that one had to take turns. As you took turns, you practiced giving and receiving. As adults, your life situations became harder to accomplish as you continued in your forgetfulness of your true divine nature each time you were hurt or in fear. It is time to empower your being again and see your life as if it were new as a child. Giving and receiving is an energetic exchange that allows the universal flow of abundance in all forms to join the show.

As you balance the giving and receiving, you open yourself up to all the abundance that the universe has to offer you. If you free your mind and ego of what you think money is, you will free yourself from any constrictions that you hold toward it.

When you want something, consider you already have it. Take pleasure in imagining how it is to have what you desire. Allow yourself to be a channel of divine, abundant grace. Gather it up and share it. Money and power are to be placed in service to others in the balance of the way. Use it for your family and others to co-create a divine space.

Removing the blocks takes clarity. Removing the blocks takes the willingness to see another way. Removing the blocks is to break the pattern. Choose that which you do not know but makes you curious. For when you are curious, you open the imagination and allow the flow of limitless opportunities into your awareness.

Imagination has no agenda, attachment, expectation, or outcome. You are in wonder and you detach enough to allow the guidance from your higher self to be heard. Be love now. Be the wonder now. See things through the eyes of the child and open to the magic and mystery that lies within. That is all.

WHOLENESS—Marrying Christ

This code allows you to reunite, you surrender the striving in seeking beyond your own heart center. Allow this code to awaken an acceleration of your true nature within you, so you may remember the vastness of who you are and see all the potentials within the conscious co-creation. In this experience, you are not alone or separate; you sense the vastness of all things, in the oneness of all things propelling you along a path of love.

By infusing this code within your mind's eye, you become One with it. Allow the power of Grace to merge and open you to the magic of Unity consciousness. This will assist you to merge all parts of yourself into the oneness again. Accept all aspects and bring love to every part of you, returning to the ONE.

CHAPTER 7
WHOLENESS

Beloved One,

To master your energy, one truly needs to find the sovereignty of the divine being within, meaning that nothing else pulls upon it to feel complete. It is an essential code of love for oneself that one truly feels no lack toward anything. When this is mastered, all abundance comes to the great knowing of the self. This union is the pure abundant energetic code of the everlasting. For one cannot be experienced without the other. That is why your journey to union is a journey of the divine self to realize that it lacks nothing and can truly be the resonance of its truest identity, no longer looking away or doubting the star within the code of One.

For magic discovered within a grain of sand is the miracle of oneness in the singularity and yet connected to the whole, fully One with the great white desert, not apart or separate, but One and connected to all. The falling away of the shackles, the burdens, the limitations you have held is the very remembrance of this unification principle captured in the moment of now. Do not doubt the star tetrahedron of discovery as it leads you to the ever now moment, for this true place is within the heart center of your very being. Your mind tries to discover how best to show the soul's code and whether the message can relate to it all. In the undoing of what was is the discovery of what is and then the message of love does sit within the pearl of wisdom. These messages of grace will surely be great.

As you journey into the deliverance of your divine nature into the physicality of All That Is, you are witnessing the tide of change within and through you, as well as through the very reality that you perceive. So, we say to you how both are interconnected. Just as two circles join, creating the vesica piscis, in the middle of the overlapping is the flame that glows and burns with the One heart of love, the One heart of God.

This new en-codement is to be your deliverance to all you have envisioned long ago. The journey of the circles to intertwine has been One of a long-lasting wisdom to come into the whole. Let now the blessings to be bestowed upon you as you continue to manifest in physical form the true divine nature of the two meeting into the whole. It has always been written and the stars do now shine as above and so below.

So now you know that all is connected within the eternal glow of everlasting unlimited divine potential. For now, potential turns into purpose and purpose is potential. The energy is gaining momentum and you are feeling the surge within you as you follow a path of discovery. It is what leads you. For you have never realized how the Divine can truly play in the magic and miracles of divine play. So, we say it is good that you play. Play within the creativity of loves fortune and fame.

GENEROSITY

GIVING THANKS FOR WHAT YOU RECEIVE

Sometimes you are so focused on what you want in your life that you do not even realize the gifts that come your way because what you are running after comes from a place of lack. This feeling of not having something creates the urge to find it and sets you on the path of searching to have what you feel you do not have.

Even though this is the trigger that sets you on the path of change, this starts the calling of transformation and the learning how to overcome the way you see things, feel them, sense them, and live them. It must also come together with the path of being thankful for what is already there and what you already have.

Please remember that the lack you feel is not there, it is a construction of your ego, your beliefs that you have overtaken throughout the experience of life your parents and society around you believed. It is in fact pure illusion. It is this that you will need to undo, day after day, to free you so that you can live the life you dream of. If we were to tell you that you have all the abundance of the great universe right before you, you too can simply say that this is pure illusion. Either way, you get to choose the life you want to live. This is the essential point we are intending to make. Believe what you are, and you will live it. What is an illusion is all that you think limits you?

What you are seeking, what you dream of, is already known inside of you. You have the idea of it, you can imagine it. If not, you would not even be trying to find it.

You already have in you what you are looking for and
you simply do not believe that this is possible. Take the
time to believe this is possible and in your body and
make it grow. This will activate it day by day, creating the
remembrance within.

If you do not take time to appreciate what life already has
given you, what you have inside of you, you then enter the
endless path of searching for something and through the
laws of attraction will attract lower vibrations of lack, making
your journey long and difficult, as you will always be looking
at your life as a struggle and in pain.

By realizing the gifts you already hold inside, you appreciate
what life gives you and allow yourself to live from the place
of grace instead of lacking and staying focused on where
you want to go. You get to be in the energy of curiosity
and wonder, which is powerful manifestation energy
because you dream your life into being. Imagination and
transformation go hand and hand as you use your creative
potential in the divine plan. Offer yourself a new existence
of a different point of view and realize that your troubles can
transform into the new.

When all seems dark, you find the light. When you venture
into the unknown, you find yourself searching for an
extraordinary meaning, but sometimes the beauty of just
living is in the everyday mundane. For when one captures
the beauty of the present moment, one can truly receive the
gifts that the simple mundane has to offer. The mundane is
only a construct because one does not allow the mundane
to be the beauty. In whatever the task, in whatever
the thought, one can stay in a never-ending pattern of

unconsciousness or focus on awareness and just be in the very presence of All That Is.

For in many times of change, one tries to go into something that seems familiar to feel the comfort you once knew, but we say that the comfort lies within your own still heart where peace dwells within you. When one becomes comfortable in their knowing, the angst starts to dissipate. Channel your thoughts into the fire and transform all you think you know. Forgive what you think you was wrong and start living with where you are pulsed to go.

In the never-ending spiral, the soul spins on the streams of time. The mystery of All That Is lives on these threads of time. The energy and the consciousness dwell into the depths of the unknown. One starts to feel the essence of their very soul. Realize the Soul dwells in the mystery. The mystery is where consciousness grows. Your consciousness will grow and grow. It will forever grow. Just as the galaxy spins and turns and changes, it grows.

For many cycles continue and some may take longer than others, but everything still dances on the same spin, and around and around you go. Where you stop, nobody knows. Come into the mystery again and if only you can accept that you are the witness of this game, then you will cease to be so serious and then start to wonder again.

You will wonder again with delight. You will wonder again in joy. For the game of life is to be en-joyed. The game of life is to be observed for you to find the true essence of the mystery within which can only be felt and not understood, for experience is the gain.

No words can tell you how for only you will know when you activate your willingness to discovery your nodes. Round and round the wheel turns. Go with the flow. The game of consciousness is that everything turns back to light. You were created in light to take flight. Everything is energy. Everything is light. You are made of everything so transform with the light.

WHAT IS BEING GENEROUS?

Most people say generosity is giving to others without counting.

We wish to make a distinction in the forms of giving. Many people give to others with the unexpressed intention of wanting to receive something in return. Very often as this generosity comes from a sense of lack, they never really receive in return what they expected and are then very frustrated and feel unloved.

Being generous starts with self, giving to you, providing for yourself, and taking care of yourself. As when you fill yourself with what you really need by allowing yourself the time to do what you soul wants you to do and by opening your heart to receive fully, nourished with what is essential to your well-being, you are then in a space of sharing with others generously without waiting for anything in return, as you already have given yourself all that your soul needs.

Beloveds, it is time to generate the energy within and through you to build more frequency and light. It is time to awaken the star stellar codes within you to this very height. The illumination of your code will be visualized as a star. You have told you before, believe us, you are a star. For the star within is the star to behold. As you fortify more of your light, generosity takes hold.

Never do you give anything away, rather it a generation of the cycles of light that you balance in the flow of the rays. From this place, there is no lack. From this place, you are the master of your light. You can manifest all that you wish. You can manifest you lover and much more bliss. Do not you see, you have thought that is so wrong. Giving is receiving as we are all the masters of this grand ball.

Come now with us and celebrate what you can generate with the mastery of light. Take time now to honor the love of your light. All that you are, all that you will ever be, is everything and more if only you believe.

Generosity
Generosity Generosity
Generosity Generosity Generosity
Generosity Generosity Generosity Generosity

Build it more and more.

THE GIFT OF BEING HUMAN

You have gone through an evolution process that makes you human. You have a reptilian brain inside, at the back of your head that is always trying to live within boundaries just like every other creature on this planet. This part of you is only concerned with surviving. However, you have developed your cortex brain, and this has brought to you the desire and longing of expansion to open to more love that provides you with a new experience on your path of evolution.

The essence of being human is that you can think, feel, understand, and experience life beyond your physical boundaries. It is a gift that evolution has given you, that which makes you different than most living creatures on this planet. Please do not forsake this. This is a precious gift.

When joy is around you, you naturally feel joyful. When pain is around you, you do not become the pain. Instead, open to compassion and enable all to transform. Hold the space for another without saying or doing anything. All you need to do is be present with your heart open to love to enable a new consciousness to emerge.

You have come to be hu-man. You have come to experience a new day. The cycle of creation is you as you ponder on the way. The journey is your liberation. Your freedom is your code, for the spirit within you is the witness to see energy manifest into a home. The home is the physical form in which you live, but also the etheric place you roam. For being human has many layers of creation to unfold.

You can access more than just the worldly in form. Being human is an experience that your soul as longed to be known. Why all the suffering? Why all the pain? To be human is to know the levels of density and darkness as well as the light and love in other planes.

Nowhere else can you experience what this place can bestow. Your soul is dedicated to this travel so that you can understand and access the code. The code of creation is unique to your very bones. Your fingerprints have a signature and so does your creation code. You have allowed the individuation of singularity to be known in the ever-present moment for you to find the at-one-ment of all.

Your very essence as a human has seeded the earth and the stars. To be human is an honor, for you are the brilliance of the stars. Where else can you experience the denser realms than on this earthly plane? Where else can you explore with love, with laughter, and with tears?

You all know the answer. You all know the pains. But with your willingness, you can be the master of this plane.

We ask you now to feel our love and know that this epic quest does not need to be done alone, for together, we can lift each other into the One heart of love for all.

BALANCE

MAKING TIME IN YOUR DAY TO DO WHAT YOUR SOUL ASKS YOU TO DO

So often, you say you do not have the time, and your ego comes to comfort you to show you that you do not have time. Life even becomes more intense as you are in a place where you feel and sense the experience of not having enough time.

Understand that you can co-create your life. If you have less time to do what your soul wants you to do, know that you are out of balance, and you will need to realign to the real you. This may bring up thoughts that this could not be true because your experience is real and there is nothing that you can do. We ask you to consider that as a co-creator you have a choice to adjust and recreate a new reality. It may take you time as you revise your plan but know that what you are seeking is the balance in an imbalanced land.

We know that this may not be easy, for the collective enforces this truth. You need a plan to sustain you. Your discipline will be to remember to come into the resonance of the holy plan. As you come in and out of balance time and time again, remember that a time will come to the zero point again.

Be gentle with yourself as your common nature as human being is to make your life hard and difficult. You have not been taught to bring love upon the self, so we ask you to practice taking the time for yourself and to transform all your fears away. Come into the observance of what it is at its core. Simply notice and make the conscious choices to restore.

By staying focused on making time for yourself and praying for this in your days, your intention will be heard throughout the cosmos and on the waves. You will listen intently to the inner wisdom and follow the guidance thus far.

Remember your soul always knows it is a living, breathing element that shines through the stars. Stop all the scurrying of wondering which way the path will or will not go. Allow the breath of living to be the elemental code.

What if the choice is never been this or that? What if you only need to arise up from the paths beyond the dark and into the light? For everything comes into rhythmic dancing of the balance of the nodes. Remember that the pause will bring you back to the presence of the day. Breathe in your life and let laughter take the day. Your Soul knows what it needs to gently bring you what you need. Stop trying to figure out things and breathe and let go of all the things.

Stop all the doubting tales and come discover the heart's delight. Face now with willingness that you are on a holy path, for you will always and forever be the co-creator of your life. It is okay if you need to refine it more; it is the journey to discovery. Whether you travel through the dark or light, it does not matter until you breathe into the knowing and clarity of your soul's breeze. Your Soul will bring you past the duality into the Oneness of All there Is.

Be gentle
Breathe in the life
Be gentle
Remember you are the light

Awaken and breathe in your life, Beloveds, for this is the pure gift at hand. No matter where you are, you will be this light. For the portal within your heart is always here with you. We are here to remind you of the beauty of all that you are. When you take the time to breathe this ever-present truth, it will not matter where you are or what you do. It will only matter that the truth of you expressed the beauty within you.

The path beyond duality is already in you. Come into the center point and you will find the ease and grace surrounding around you. Taking the time for your Soul to be is all that is needed to do. If you allow this willingness to be part of your existence, you will come into a place of merging the many aspects of you.

Light and dark
Right and left
Sound and Silence
Become ONE
The polarities do arise
And transform into Light

So many people will give you the formula. Let the mind fall
away and let your thoughts of "should" and "should not"
be gone. Simply be your greatest self within the moments
of the breath. That is all. All is that. Together you climb
into the sun. That is all. All is that. Together you feel the
embrace of love.

You are the One
The special, special One
All the elements
Swirl into the One
Making all the elements
Rising into the One
You may not know
Which way to go
Should I stay or should I go?
Open to this love
Feel this lasting love
Be in this love
Then love will show you which way to go
Creation now does fill with light
Creation now does fill with love
All is a cycle that goes around and around the sun

BALANCING BODY, MIND AND SPIRIT

It is essential to put your mind at rest and slow down its activity. The mind is always trying to find solutions, analyzing the level of stress in the body and tries to find a way to calm any anxiety or fear that is held within. When the level of stress is high, the mind automatically thinks that the body is in danger, and it will start to spin, accelerating the thoughts to find a solution to help the body find its balance again.

This leads into a frenetic and destructive spiral where the mind spins around and around, accelerating throughout the hours of the day, disturbing your days and nights, and making things agitated inside your physical body and creating dis-ease.

Many people talk about taming the mind and focusing on positive ideas. These various techniques do not sustain as the mind is reacting to a stress that is in the body. As you free the stress that is trapped in the physical body, you will free the mind and it will come to rest.

By using the movement to release the stress in the body, you balance the body that will then balance the mind.

A lot of people use sports to help the body find its center. This method is through the doing, pushing the body, releasing hormones that make you feel good. If you push your body too hard, the balanced cannot be sustained because the body may be injured by the repetitive stress.

What we strongly suggest are physical movements with your eyes closed. Why is that? It is because you will allow your body to move from the inside. Your body is a living library that stocks all unbalanced energies. When there is imbalance, the body aches and pain provide the signal. By taking time every morning to move into your un-ease, slowly, by breathing and moving to stretch, following the inner wisdom of your body, you release all tensions; you balance your body from the inside.

By allowing your inner wisdom to move you out of the blockages, you allow the grace of love to release the unbalanced energies stored inside. By staying inside with your eyes closed, you follow the graceful dance of your body. You take time to connect with yourself on the inside. You open to your intuition and allow your inner guidance to show you the way out of your inner stress.

This will help you to take care and to listen to your needs. You will know that you hold inside a profound wisdom that can guide you. You will connect with yourself from the inside and allow your spirit to show you the way. Your body is very powerful. It is organically made to find its own balance if you allow it to do so. In return you will feel better, and your body will be balanced and your mind free. You will learn how to be more present in the moment, providing a whole new world of experiences.

By allowing time every morning to dance from the inside and to breathe and move with grace, you will feel loved, happy, and will witness the change in your entire life experience. You will allow spirit to shine through you, gifting the beauty of love and fulfillment to humanity.

The heart portal sings a song. Bring in the chimes. Bring in the noise. Allow the harmony to open its doors. Bring in the child. Bring in the sun. All will balance into the One. All will balance into the One.

Oh, my Beloveds, the story of the new you are ready to be balanced within you. Oh, my Beloveds, the awakening is here. Walk now in courage to be clear. Walk now in courage to see what is nearby.

Show all your colors. Stand in the light. Come toward the mother and open to her light. She has the love now, as the father does stand tall. He knows the mother is always here to bestow. For creation is always waiting for the father to bring forth his light. Creation is the Mother, and the action is the father, and the child will shine the brilliance of this holy light.

What is balance? How can you find this in times of chaos, drama, and struggle? It does take a willingness to be bold and to be disciplined into the heart of One. For discipline is knowledge and with action it is bestowed. The wisdom turns to courage and then all creates a new road.

A new stream of consciousness is waiting to be birthed within the shadows it hovers and is waiting to shine more. In the darkest hours and when your mind likes to judge, open instead into the heart and watch the sunlight.

Be the feeling of the birth and not the pain of restriction. For the birth is the freedom when one balances its aspects to nurture the mind, the body, and spirit. The alignment of these things will bring forth new creations with ease and flow. The struggle comes when one is neglected, and the others run the show.

LIVING IN PRESENCE

Living in presence is your divine nature. You are Presence. You were born in presence and if you look at the eyes of a newborn, you see the presence in total surrender.

And yet you spend your life thinking you are not divine and attached to your physical self. We are here you say that you are on the path of evolution, but it is only the path of coming back home to your divine nature. Through your practice to retrieve your truth, you come in and out of presence. To find the balance in your emotions, be present in the holy instant. This will help you to step out of drama. Emotions come and go; do not attach to them, you cannot stop them, but you can learn to surrender to them by allowing them to flow and move through you. Your body will restore to balance once you allow the e-motion to pass.

Be free in the mind by allowing thoughts to pass by practicing living in the present moment and fully engaged, giving all your attention to the now. By being in profound gratitude, this is something that comes by itself; it will emerge by itself in your days when you live in presence, it will immerge inside and outside.

Ask for the assistance of the Divine to help you to be fully present in the now and to live through the higher frequencies of love. Allow your true nature to be present. Allow your light to radiate on this earth, knowing profoundly inside the perfection that you are. Allow yourself to see your essence and choose that it is now time for all of YOU to be present in your existence!

Everything that you are is breath. BREATHE, Beloveds, breathe in the breath of life, this is the creation energy of the life force in which you have come to live. Focus on your breath. Let your thoughts fall away. Focus on your breath. Let your thoughts fall away. We repeat ourselves for you to understand the creation of your patterns. When you bring awareness to your patterns, you understand when you act in consciousness and when you act unconsciously. The awareness alone is the liberation, for all you must do is focus on awareness. Focus on the breath that moves through your body and how it sustains your living organs and cells.

Often the things we dismiss or take for granted are the very things that can liberate us from the pain and suffering we experience. For life is filled with paradoxes and the mystery is at play. We ask you not to understand with the lower mind, but rather experience it throughout your cells, for the grounding aspect of your humanness allows the magic to be at play.

Your very presence is the magic of love. Your very presence is the Star. Your very presence holds the power you seek, as you understand that you are the Master within the Star.

PHYSICAL STRENGTH

LETTING MORE OF YOUR LIGHT COME THROUGH

When the human self-aligns to the cosmos, the bridge to the higher dimensions is formed. You stop going around in circles through your emotions and your mind. You surrender deeply in the body.

When you let more of your light to come through, you open your entire human self. All the parts that compose of your human self, all the various bodies, all the facets of your diamond, unify and become ONE. You are limitless, unbounded, aligned with the Universe. As the light pours through you, all is in alignment with the cosmos and you are free to connect with the higher vibrations that pour through you to enliven more and more this human body, allowing more and more light to shine, becoming a beacon of light.

This fulfillment creates an everlasting sense of having the universe living inside. As you align your physical biology with creation, you then feel invisible, eternal, and full in your co-creator potential.

To live this experience, it is something that you grow into. It does not happen overnight, it does not happen when you want, it happens when all inside is at ease. The whole process of allowing this change to happen, the learning day after day to love the self-more and more, allows you to open your heart, mind, and soul, bridging filaments of light that braid with one another that creates experience after experience of powerful connections.

We wish to remind you, when you are in states of doubt, that every light connection that you do, is eternal and is stored within you. It does not disappear when you enter again in a state of separation, doubt, or wounding in the spiral of the karma. It stays connected, waiting for you to build the next connection, so that they may braid and become more powerful.

So, we urge you to commit day after day, to your path of learning and become more conscious of you, through the feeling of the body. As it is through this physical body, your human self that you will find balance and peace within.

Follow into the sun
The path of light is on the run
Run with me into the sun
Now you will find the bursting life of love
You are the sun
Shining bright
Come into knowing you are the light
Birth the magic through
Come into the circle of blue
The child spins into grace now
The laughter fills your body too
Swirling and twirling
You spin anew
It fills you
The light of you
So, swirl and swirl the magic through
It will imbue you
The fun of life is here for you
If you believe it is true
If you know this through
It will come through you
Something fills your heart
Following into stars
Opening filling with the Grace
Following the path
Following the path
Come now—into the circle
Follow the path of the light
Come now, spin me a twirl now
Follow the child into the light

Follow me
Friends come into the square
You hold hands
You are the pair
Round and around you spin on the thread of light
Holding the heart's desire of life

How you have forgotten all that you are. You are the light of One. Do not despair. You are a channel of light. We are here to remind you that you have come from the stars and you are here to bring forth the beauty and wisdom of these stars.

Everything is connected; as the sun does shine, so do you. When you start to remember your star stellar essence, you begin a journey of light. All that you were and all that you are spins on the conscious threads of light that you hold. For we have heard all your prayers. We have heard all your wishes and dreams and you thread them throughout the cosmos for your manifestations to take hold on your worldly plane.

You have never been forgotten. You are always here with us. We always send you the love of the creator into your breath, into the life that you are living, into all that you are. We ask you to share this awareness with us and spread this message to all, through your thoughts, through the loving of the earth, through the blessings of the waters. For your natural world feels your vibrations. The natural world is a symbiotic life thread of your co-creations, your thoughts, and your actions. You are surrounded by many blessings, if only you connect with your consciousness and bring life into the world with this perspective. You are love and life, Dear Ones. You are love and life.

The mastery of self has brought you to a place beyond
the gifts that you seek. All the codes of One have been
given to you from long ago. You are now bringing forth
the remembrance of your soul plus the experience you
have gained within the nodes. For creation consciousness
develops day to day as you bring forth the awareness
of the day.

Many timelines stream into One as you align into the sun.
The sun is your Christ. The Christ is the crystalline nature of
light. Beloved Ones, to be the bearer of One's heart is to
lay down the doubt that you do not have enough. It is to
lay down the burdens of what you think you need to do and
instead arise into the beauty of you.

We have given you this message time and time again, but
you will need to be reminded of this just the same. For
many, many times do you forget your code of light. So
many, many times will we remind you of this light. Forgotten
it may be, but we will never be the forgetful one who
doubts thee. We are the Ones who will always sing the song
of great love and great songs.

We are here to bring forth the message that allows you
to birth this new day for all to co-create this new way.
The creation element of wonder is afoot, and we now
bring you the deliverance that you would bring into your
manifestations. Many of you have heard the call of your
heart's desires and you try to figure out the best way
to express this in physical form. But when your passion
ceases because you forget the wonder, you start again to
rediscover the feeling you felt when the inspiration arose,
and then will you try to reclaim this mode.

Moving within the mysterious tides of creation is the essence of knowing the magic of creation. It is nothing to understand in the moment at hand, only to move with the energy of e-motion. Your feelings have been under-utilized. You have used them to justify your sorrows. Instead, we ask you to run into the sorrow and finally collapse into the meadow where the sun can send it is living rays upon you to then again fill up with inspiration that you bring forth a brighter tomorrow. For whatever the emotion it will be the access point of creation, use this energy to co-create with your passion. This Beloved is aligning to you light that brings consciousness to your life. You will forever be and always will be the creation aspect of love's pure delight.

When you were created into form, your consciousness knew it would be swarmed with many indicators of this and that. You knew you would need to sift through all the crap to find the truest of intentions and not just something on the level of the devil. What you want that you cannot have comes from the essence of something that you crave. The light is abundant, it has no restrictions, so turn into the river of many, many depictions. For your soul will create time and time again. It has many avenues to walk upon the land. Know the paths will combine and intertwine. The spiral will go round and around and into the journey you will go within.

We love you. We embrace you with the life's tender kiss.

CONNECTING YOUR HEART TO YOUR HEAD

One of your most common unconscious reactions is to start judging, and this comes from your level of fear.

Offering a vibration that matches your desires rather
than matching the vibration that is for you to choose. We
are here to inspire you to create a new experience that
matches what you want to create to a more loving and
compassionate experience and thus, feeling, knowing, and
experiencing how it is when you live there, bringing this into
the now to radiate it out. In your present state of *beingness*,
you will create what you call your future.

As your e-motions are constantly affecting how your brain
responds chemically and guides the body, it is crucial to
strengthen the connection between you heart and your
head. When doing this meditation, it is important to know
that sometimes you may feel things and sometimes may
not. We ask you now to focus on feeling, focus on relaxing
and being present; the energy works whether you feel
it or not.

Understand that you heart sends far more information
to your brain then the other way around. You can bathe
your brain with the love of the heart. As your heart is a
multidimensional gateway, it opens your brain to reconnect
with the multiverse.

So, please shut your eyes and relax…

Beloveds, as you breathe, breathe into the space of love.
Focus on your heart center and relax you mind. Allow your
thoughts to float away and breathe. Breathe deeply. Feel
the weight of your body. Feel the clothes on your skin.
Allow your hearing to be wide and open. Fully feel your
senses and breathe.

The mind and the heart work together in a dance. The awareness of the rhythm between the two is your task as you open to receive the e-motions of the heart, you consciously tell the lower mind to relax. You tell the lower mind that you forgive it for the thoughts of doubt and fear, for you are breathing into your heart center and giving your mind what it needs to unwind.

Allow the pause of the present moment to bring you back to you, the authentic part of you that allows your feelings of fear, doubt, and shame to be honored by the heart. Open your heart more as the mind can relax into the frequency of this new opening of love.

This will take practice. For the consistency of this practice will create a pattern or a new code within you to be in balance and access the mysteries of light to work in your favor to manifest the gift that you are—the true you of love.

MANAGING YOUR ENERGY BODY— YOUR PRECIOUS RESOURCE

The first thing that is essential to be in good health is to breathe. This might make you smile, but so many people do not know how to breathe. So, let us take a moment to learn how to breathe.

Place your hand on your belly and push your belly outwards as you breath in. Allow your upper body to be filled by the breath. Imagine the breath going into your shoulders as it opens through the back of your upper body. Breathe in this place more and more and more, without needing to hold your breath.

Then with the outbreath, bring the breath to the front of your body, your shoulders, the front of your upper body, into your belly, and contracting the belly as if it could touch your spine.

Continue for at least five minutes.

The second is being conscious of what you eat. You need to understand that what you eat is information. Through the chewing process, the information is being released into your stomach, also called your second brain. Your food is instructing your body, so you are what you eat. To integrate this is a long process, it will probably take you time, and nevertheless, we encourage you to reflect on it.

The third is to move the body. However, you choose to do this is of no importance. Allow your body to move according to your innate intelligence by closing your eyes to go within. Allow the body to move so that it may release the stored e-motions. Take care of yourself through the movement, whatever the rhythm of the moment, and allow the body to express and release to experience more freedom in your body as well as a sense of well-being.

The fourth is to manage your thoughts and emotions that create the energy in which you are living. The body can store for some time any imbalance, but eventually it will release what has been taken in to make place for the new. This happens when your body feels safe enough to liberate and heal whatever needs to be done. It comes from your creations of the past and your need to acknowledge that your body is repairing the excess of negative thoughts and emotions that polluted the body. To prevent this, we encourage you to stay aligned and become conscious of the thoughts and emotions you carry, freeing them so that the body does not need to store anything for you.

Your immune system is essential for your good health. One of the major entering points is located just behind your thymus chakra, also called your higher heart, just behind the sternum, the two bones just under the throat. By tapping this region softly, you can activate your immune system that will help you stay healthy.

1. Please tap softly, imagine, and feel and say out loud, "I activate my immune system through all the vault nodules and lymph nodes, sending the information that I am safe and open to heal any imbalance that might be in place. I forgive myself for any experience of fear and suffering," imagine and feel, take your time.

2. "I ask for forgiveness from any other being that I might have hurt or that might have hurt me," imagine and feel, take your time.

3. "I send love and appreciation to myself and all others concerned," imagine and feel, take your time. Allow all your organs and cells to receive this information. Take time with this process.

Your nervous system feels it is made of fibers of light that allow the information to come through. You need to take care of yourself so that your body can be ready to receive the new energies that are being pored through by your source of creation. We encourage you to nourish yourself, emotionally, physically, mentally, and spiritually through your awareness, with love and kindness. Actively have the intention of releasing the past and to allow a rewiring to occur with your universal consciousness, according to your truth.

The heart of the universal human, infinite love is within each and every one of you. Choose to connect to your heart, honoring One another, as each one brings your unique contribution to the human evolution. Everyone is raising their frequencies to create stars of light around the world; the environment is cleaning up, giving the planet time to breath.

Choose to continue to evolve. Be ready to make the change and go to the next level. You are born of the earth and born of the stars, universal human you are.

Take good care of yourself. Take good care of your body. Allow the rhythms of the tides to show you what you are made up of and allow the energy in motion to move through you without judging it and labeling it as a single point of you.

As you manage your energetic system, know that there are many levels and layers to your vast *beingness*. Once you understand the expansiveness of your consciousness, you start to allow your curiosity of developing an intimate relationship with you. This intimate relationship will give you the seeds of wonder to draw upon and allow new growth to come through you.

No need to make this hard, Beloveds, just know your higher self will guide the way. The diligence you need is to create and fortify this relationship with the self. Not in naming or labeling, but in discovering of the self. If you allow yourself the gentleness of heart, you will allow the energetic flow of creation to move through your consciousness creating more opportunities as you access the unlimited potential of creation.

We are here to seed your consciousness with the inspiration to discover more of yourself through the codes that you create and hold. We are here to allow you the support that you need, that when you are ready to receive, we are here indeed.

For all we know is nothing in a sense because we are constantly creating and doing our best—our best to evolve no matter the stance, for we know the soul will always and forever grow, grow, grow. Understand that your divine blueprint has the power to recreate the life you have always desired. When you need to release and restore, do this with love and open the doors. Clean your windows and uncover the shelves and start a build a new home for the Beloved instead.

ANCHOR PEACE AND HARMONY

CHANGING YOUR LIFE BY LOVING YOUR BODY

Your physical body is the vessel that contains all the memories of the present and past experiences, may it be on the earth or elsewhere. All is referenced precisely in your body; it is stored deeply in all your tissues and systems. Your body is radiating a certain frequency that, through the law of attraction, is calling in your daily experience.

That is why it is so important to bring more love into your physical body as this will change your life experience, by

attracting more love, allowing the love to pour through all
your cells.

So, take a moment to breathe deeply. Breathe in and
out and allow the breath of life to calm you completely,
releasing all that can be released, through the outbreath.

Close your eyes and enter the darkness, into the field of all.
Notice that you are in this place or all potential all the time.
You only see it when you close your eyes, even though it is
always around you.

Allow yourself to enter this field of the void, allow you to
expand, and your consciousness opens, limitlessly. Allow
yourself to go far out, all around you, in this never-ending
expansion process.

Then call in the highest conscious part of yourself, this
cosmic energy that is your essence. Let yourself connect
deeply, by tapping into this consciousness and allow it to
feed you with the energy of love. Allow this magnificent
energy of creation to flood through as you open. You need
to consciously call it in to receive it, as you are the guardian
of your free will and nothing can come through if you do
not call for it. So consciously say out loud, "bring me more
love," and memorize this experience with all your senses.
Let it come in.

Now open your body, allow love to nourish all your cells,
allow yourself to feel loved. Allow yourself to be loved,
allow yourself to feel worthy of being loved. Allow yourself
to be proud of your body. Thank your body for being this
magnificent vessel filled with the codes of love.

Be love, be in love with yourself! Love yourself in the same way you wish to be loved!

Allow your body to radiate love, to attract more loving experiences in your life!

BELONGING

When you feel connected to the others and find the place where you fit, you feel powerful. This feeling of togetherness is an immense creative power than can achieve much more than doing things on our own.

This merging with collective consciousness initiates a major shift, it is of the most importance to achieve wellness, and good health as even our immune system is boosted by a sense of belonging.

The need to belong is to feel connected deeply with the collective consciousness, which will provide you with all the strength of the group, helping you to fit in the human family.

You often have memories that disconnect you from your family, friends, and humanity as a whole. The usual patterns of separation tend to make you feel less or more than another, you compare yourself with others, you might even have the sense of not belonging and of being different.

This, in a way, is true as everyone is unique in the gift he or her brings to the earth, through the seeding of your essence in the heart of Mother Earth, in the light you gift to her soul.

Nevertheless, you are a collective consciousness that is deeply connected through the experience of the human race on the planet. Nobody is here for nothing, neither can he or she be replaced by another; every individual is bringing something precious to the collective consciousness that is in the process of evolution.

It is true that through your physical eyes, limited by the density of the illusion, having forgotten who you really are, where you come from, what has been your cosmic journey, and what you are here to achieve, you can easily be mistaken. Nevertheless, in your deepest heart you hold the knowing that you are One with creation and you belong to a bigger family, connected with what might be call your star family.

Here again, we wish to explain, that your family on the earth is part of your star family, as so often you disconnect thinking that you do not belong. You experience through the human form with souls that are deeply connected to you, and here, again, nothing is unorganized. You are surrounded by souls that have evolutionary contracts with you, so you may learn and evolve, so that the entire consciousness may transform and create a more loving experience on the planet.

That is why, we urge you to see the beauty that your family members, friends hold for you. The learning through the mirror they are just for you. They play out all that you refuse to accept as being part of you, all that you judge and wish to put away, and that keeps on coming back over and over again.

So, start thanking them deeply, understand that they will remain by your side until you integrate the teaching, they have come to share with you, heal the separation that you have created, the burdens you have stored in your physical body and life experience. This does not have to be done in a second; it is a process that will unfold on itself, it cannot be rushed, it cannot just be understood, it needs to be lived, experienced deeply in the now.

But, have faith, by choosing to reconnect, to love yourself so that you may love others just in the way they are, in the way they think, act, and speak. Understanding that there is a purpose to their experience on a collective level, even if you do not understand why this is taking place. Everyone has a piece to play and not all are easy to live.

Allow yourself to feel that you belong to your family and that your place and experience is as precious as the ones of others. Accept that all is perfectly orchestrated by a divine purpose that goes beyond your understanding. Remember that you are part of the whole and that you are precious in so many ways and participating in the big wave of transformation, lifting the collective consciousness to an entire new level, so that all can live more harmony, joy, and love.

To be able to belong, accept foremost yourselves. By living in the now, you open to what is.

MERGING—THE THREE-FOLD FLAME

Merging divine will and divine love, merging of all lower bodies, creating the integration of your light body will allow you to see divine perfection as nothing else exists anymore, you transcend the human experience, you go beyond, you are back home.

Your crown chakra opens the door to your enlightenment, anchoring the higher heavens on the earth. To work toward its opening, clear your mental and emotional bodies through the highest levels of bliss, and connect to unity consciousness, enabling you to be the rainbow bridge to higher realms. This is a process, and it cannot be rushed or forced; it is through the resolving of the karma in the lower charkas, the balancing of polarities, that allow the full awakening of the Christ consciousness.

When you are connected with the wisdom of your heart, the sacred chambers that lie within, it will blossom, enabling you to attain the highest level of service. The more you focus on the great return to love, the more your body will transform and allow you to hold a higher amount of light, allowing you to experience a higher truth of wholeness to create your reality.

Beloveds, we have reminded you to balance your energies of the polarities. When the force of this balance is held within, you create the mysteries of light to ignite the flame within your heart gateway to move the energies around you, through you and into the collective vastness of all there is.

This movement is your energetic code that you are sharing with the world, the master co-creator working within the realms of light that utilizes the three-fold flame within the heart of all creation. For everything we say and remind you is only a symbolic message to activate the codes within you. Do not worry if the understanding of the mind is not fully known; just know that you are receiving the codes of creation within you.

Everything is a paradox as the energies of polarities at work. In the realms of light and all creation, the surrendering to the lower mind is the willingness to know that you do not know but have the courage to discover and move through it.

Be the bearer of your own truth as you masterfully awaken your heart's truth. This is the only beginning and ending of all—to be your own fulfillment of the love for all.

The motion and doing will access the creation in the physical. The three-fold flame of light utilized in the day and night will help anchor a new beginning of a life that is worth living. For everyone and everything will hold higher light of creation. The frequency of what you knew is upgrading into a new octave to begin anew.

Create, Beloveds, create within the light of day. Create in the realms of night in your dreams and follow along them as you wake, for you will surely discover more as the pieces of the puzzle that you do explore will come into oneness again and again as you build upon foundations again and again.

The structures you create now will be the foundations you will live again in your future. For everything in all time will be masterfully co-created in the now.

The adventure has begun. The adventure is here. What will you build? What will you dream?

ABOUT THE AUTHORS

Naomi Fay is an author, progressive educator, and spiritual leader. Her mission is to live an authentic life to model for her children and for humanity by bringing the Divine Feminine codes of love, wisdom, and co-creation.

Nathalie Moutia is an author, an experienced divine wisdom channel, artwork artist, teacher, and healer.

Her mission is to assist all benevolent beings to anchor their light in the core of Mother Gaia so that they may fulfill their souls' life purpose by living their gifts and assisting humanity to live in unity consciousness.

Mango Publishing, established in 2014, publishes an eclectic list of books by diverse authors—both new and established voices—on topics ranging from business, personal growth, women's empowerment, LGBTQ studies, health, and spirituality to history, popular culture, time management, decluttering, lifestyle, mental wellness, aging, and sustainable living. We were recently named 2019 *and* 2020's #1 fastest growing independent publisher by *Publishers Weekly.* Our success is driven by our main goal, which is to publish high quality books that will entertain readers as well as make a positive difference in their lives.

Our readers are our most important resource; we value your input, suggestions, and ideas. We'd love to hear from you—after all, we are publishing books for you!

Please stay in touch with us and follow us at:

Facebook: Mango Publishing
Twitter: @MangoPublishing
Instagram: @MangoPublishing
LinkedIn: Mango Publishing
Pinterest: Mango Publishing
Newsletter: mangopublishinggroup.com/newsletter

Join us on Mango's journey to reinvent publishing, one book at a time.

CPSIA information can be obtained
at www.ICGtesting.com
Printed in the USA
JSHW052146250421
13780JS00003B/3

9 781642 504491